A REPORT OF THE CSIS
DEFENSE-INDUSTRIAL
INITIATIVES GROUP

Asian Defense Spending, 2000–2011

Project Directors
David J. Berteau
Guy Ben-Ari

Authors
Joachim Hofbauer
Priscilla Hermann
Sneha Raghavan

October 2012

50 YEARS | *CHARTING* OUR FUTURE

CSIS | CENTER FOR STRATEGIC & INTERNATIONAL STUDIES

About CSIS—50th Anniversary Year

For 50 years, the Center for Strategic and International Studies (CSIS) has developed practical solutions to the world's greatest challenges. As we celebrate this milestone, CSIS scholars continue to provide strategic insights and bipartisan policy solutions to help decisionmakers chart a course toward a better world.

CSIS is a bipartisan, nonprofit organization headquartered in Washington, D.C. The Center's more than 200 full-time staff and large network of affiliated scholars conduct research and analysis and develop policy initiatives that look to the future and anticipate change.

Since 1962, CSIS has been dedicated to finding ways to sustain American prominence and prosperity as a force for good in the world. After 50 years, CSIS has become one of the world's preeminent international policy institutions focused on defense and security; regional stability; and transnational challenges ranging from energy and climate to global development and economic integration.

Former U.S. senator Sam Nunn has chaired the CSIS Board of Trustees since 1999. John J. Hamre became the Center's president and chief executive officer in 2000. CSIS was founded by David M. Abshire and Admiral Arleigh Burke.

CSIS does not take specific policy positions; accordingly, all views expressed herein should be understood to be solely those of the author(s).

Cover photo credits: NASA Visible Earth catalog.

ISBN 978-0-89206-753-4

Center for Strategic and International Studies
1800 K Street, N.W.
Washington, D.C. 20006
Tel: (202) 887-0200
Fax: (202) 775-3119
Web: www.csis.org

Table of Contents

List of Figures

List of Tables

Executive Summary

Asia is growing in geostrategic importance. Despite the financial crisis that began in 2008, many Asian countries experienced relatively less fiscal distress and increased their level of involvement in global affairs. Indicative of the region's elevated global role is the United States' pivot toward the Asia-Pacific region as outlined in the Strategic Guidance recently released by the Department of Defense.[1] With Asian defense spending projected to overtake that of Europe by the end of 2012, the United States' posture rebalancing toward the Asia-Pacific region is likely to continue.[2]

Today, several Asian countries are already among the largest defense spenders in the world. In addition, unlike the defense budgets in many other regions, Asian defense spending continues to be on the rise. This trend stands in particularly stark contrast to Europe and the United States, where defense budgets have been declining in recent years.

The analysis in this report presents key budgetary trends for the five countries with the largest defense budgets in Asia[3]—China, India, Japan, South Korea, and Taiwan—for the years 2000 to 2011.[4, 5] In 2011, these countries collectively spent an approximate $224 billion (in constant 2011 U.S. dollars) on defense. The first chapter of the report provides a cross-country comparison of key defense budgetary trends for the five Asian countries in total and per-soldier defense spending terms. The second chapter presents an in-depth analysis of defense spending in each country. It discusses total and per-soldier spending trends and provides a breakdown of defense spending by functional categories: Defense Investment, which includes procurement, military construction, and research and development (R&D); Personnel, and Operation and Maintenance (O&M). For India, Japan, and South Korea, the country analysis also includes a breakdown of the Defense Investment category into Defense R&D and Defense Procurement. The third chapter provides a cross-country assessment of the defense spending trends in the five countries by comparing budget breakdowns into functional defense spending categories. The fourth chapter presents the findings of this report and outlines areas for future study. An appendix provides a detailed description of the methodology used to collect and analyze the data for this report.

The analysis in this report yields the following two key findings:

Finding 1. Accelerated Growth in Defense Spending

Defense spending increased in all five Asian countries between 2000 and 2011. Per-soldier defense spending followed similar trajectories in all countries but Taiwan due to relatively stable force structures. However, the increases in defense budgets did not occur in a linear manner. Instead, growth in defense spending visibly accelerated around 2005; with the exception of South Korea, growth rates

---

[1] Department of Defense (DoD), "Sustaining U.S. Global Leadership: Priorities for 21st Century Defense," January 2012, http://www.defense.gov/news/Defense_Strategic_Guidance.pdf.

[2] International Institute for Strategic Studies, "Military Balance 2012—Press Statement," March 7, 2012, http://www.iiss.org/publications/military-balance/the-military-balance-2012/press-statement/.

[3] See the Methodology section for the geographical definition applied for this ranking.

[4] The total annual defense expenditures for Japan include expenditures for U.S. forces stationed in Japan, but they exclude expenditures related to the Special Action Committee on Okinawa, as well as U.S. force realignment expenditures. For South Korea, the total defense expenditures include costs for relocating U.S. forces to South Korea.

[5] CSIS acknowledges that Taiwan's legal status is contested. For the purposes of the report, it is referred to as a country for ease of comparison with the four other countries analyzed.

(when measured in constant 2011 U.S. dollars) have been higher between 2005 and 2011 than between 2000 and 2005.

Future defense spending trends will hinge primarily on political and economic circumstances. Continued or even increasing tensions in the security and political landscape of the Asia-Pacific region would constitute a stimulus for further increases in defense spending. However, security policy considerations only provide the motive for sustaining growth in defense spending. The key enabler will be the availability of financial resources. Should the economic climate in the region continue to develop positively, many countries will have the means to respond to their security concerns by further increasing their defense budgets, possibly at an accelerated pace. On the other hand, if the future financial environment proves to be more austere, pressure on defense spending will also mount.

Finding 2. Prioritizing Quantity, not Quality

While overall defense budgets of the five Asian countries are quite substantial, per-soldier defense spending is not (with the exception of Japan's). The underlying reason for this marked difference between total and per-soldier defense spending is the extensive force structures sustained by all countries but Japan in relation to the size of their overall defense budget.

Per-soldier defense spending constitutes a proxy variable for force quality as it measures the total resources available for recruiting, training, compensating, equipping, and sustaining an individual soldier. The comparatively low levels of per-soldier spending in four of the top five Asian spenders therefore raises questions about the extent to which these countries prioritize the size of their armed forces over their quality.

It remains to be seen whether China, India, South Korea, and Taiwan will continue on this trajectory or if they will eventually follow trends observed in Europe and the United States, where force structure has been reduced considerably in favor of higher-quality forces. Ample trade space is certainly available in China, India, and South Korea. Yet security, economic, and other political considerations might make this course of action unviable for the foreseeable future.

Figure I below presents key defense trends in Asia and illustrates the above-mentioned findings:

Figure I. Key Asian Defense Trends (2000–2011)

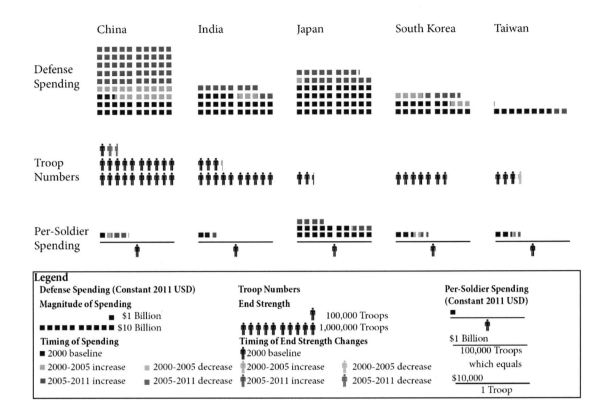

Sources: Chinese MoD White Papers, China's National Defense, 2002, 2004, 2006, 2008, 2010; U.S. Department of Defense 2010 Annual Report to Congress on Military and Security Developments Involving the People's Republic of China; Indian Union Budget and Economic Survey: Expenditure Budget, 2000–2013; Japanese MoD White Papers, 2005–2011; South Korean MoD White Papers, 2000, 2006, 2008, 2010; South Korean MoD; Taiwanese National Defense Report, 2009 and 2011; IISS Military Balance; analysis by CSIS Defense-Industrial Initiatives Group.

1. Asian Defense Spending Trends (2000–2011)

The analysis in this chapter presents key budgetary trends for the five Asian countries in total and per-soldier defense spending terms for the years 2000 to 2011. To allow for a more accurate comparison of the growth trajectories in the individual countries, this chapter also provides an overview of indexed defense spending trends in constant 2011 U.S. dollars and in local currencies.

1.1 Total Defense Spending

The five Asian countries analyzed in this report—China, India, Japan, South Korea, and Taiwan—spent a combined $224 billion on defense in 2011 (see Figure 1.1 below).[1] In constant 2011 U.S. dollars, this equates to almost twice the amount spent by these five countries in 2000. To capture only real effects, all spending in this report is assessed on a constant 2011 U.S. dollar basis unless otherwise noted.

Figure 1.1 provides a cross-country comparison of total defense spending for the time period 2000–2011.

Figure 1.1. Total Defense Spending by Country (2000–2011)

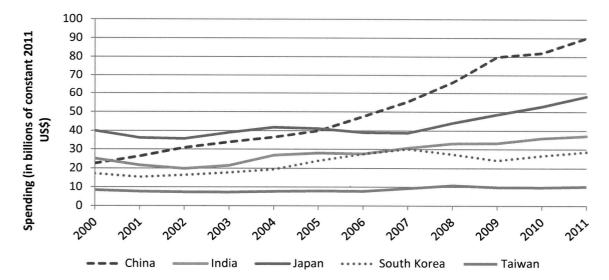

Sources: Chinese MoD White Papers, China's National Defense, 2002, 2004, 2006, 2008, 2010; U.S. Department of Defense 2010 Annual Report to Congress on Military and Security Developments Involving the People's Republic of China; Indian Union Budget and Economic Survey: Expenditure Budget, 2000–2013; Japanese MoD White Papers, 2005–2011; South Korean MoD White Papers, 2000, 2006, 2008, 2010; South Korean MoD; Taiwanese National Defense Report, 2009 and 2011; analysis by CSIS Defense-Industrial Initiatives Group.

Until 2005, Japan had the largest defense budget in Asia. Since 2005, China has been the biggest spender on defense, having previously replaced India as the second-biggest spender in 2001. This comparatively rapid expansion in defense spending is also illustrated by China's share of the group's combined defense spending, which more than doubled from 19.9 percent in 2000 to 40.2 percent in 2011.

---

[1] See the Methodology section for a detailed discussion of sources used and data analysis techniques applied.

Regarding China, it should be noted that the analysis in this section is based on the official Chinese defense budgets. Many analysts posit that Chinese official sources do not capture Chinese defense spending in its entirety. These analysts propose instead alternative, higher estimates of Chinese defense spending.[2] The in-depth analysis of China's defense budget in Section 1.2 of this report discusses some of these alternative estimates.

Figure 1.2 provides a cross-country comparison of indexed changes in total defense spending with 2000 as the base year, for the time period 2000–2011.

Figure 1.2. Indexed Total Defense Spending in Constant 2011 U.S. Dollars by Country (2000–2011)

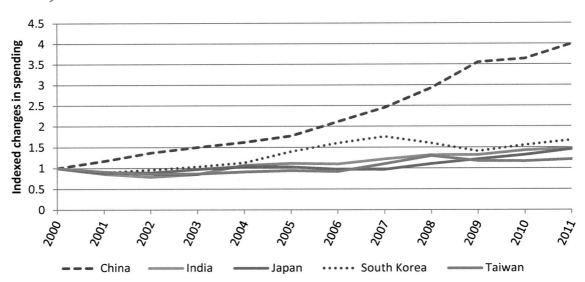

Sources: Chinese MoD White Papers, China's National Defense, 2002, 2004, 2006, 2008, 2010; U.S. Department of Defense 2010 Annual Report to Congress on Military and Security Developments Involving the People's Republic of China; Indian Union Budget and Economic Survey: Expenditure Budget, 2000–2013; Japanese MoD White Papers, 2005–2011; South Korean MoD White Papers, 2000, 2006, 2008, 2010; South Korean MoD; Taiwanese National Defense Report, 2009 and 2011; analysis by CSIS Defense-Industrial Initiatives Group.

Total defense spending for all five countries has been increasing in constant 2011 U.S. dollars over the last decade. However, the growth rates among the five Asian countries have not been uniform. A more accurate comparison of the growth in Asian defense budgets involves viewing defense spending in constant 2011 U.S. dollars indexed to the year 2000 (see Figure 1.2) and the compounded annual growth rates (CAGRs) of defense spending (see Table 1). This comparison shows that between 2000 and 2011, China's defense spending increased at the highest rate, with an 11-year CAGR of 13.4 percent. South Korea was the second fastest growing defense spender during that period, with a 4.8 percent CAGR. India and Japan were on a very similar growth trajectory, with 3.6 and 3.5 percent CAGRs, respectively. Taiwan experienced the lowest increase in defense spending among the group with a CAGR of 1.8 percent.

---

[2] See, for instance, Stockholm International Peace Research Institute (SIPRI), "SIPRI Military Expenditure Database, 2011," http://www.sipri.org/databases/milex.

Table 1. CAGRs for Total Defense Spending in Constant 2011 U.S. Dollars by Country (2000–2011)

Countries	Defense Spending CAGR		
	2000–2005	2005–2011	2000–2011
China	12.1%	14.5%	13.4%
India	2.2%	4.8%	3.6%
Japan	0.6%	6.0%	3.5%
South Korea	6.9%	3.0%	4.8%
Taiwan	-1.2%	4.3%	1.8%

Sources: Chinese MoD White Papers, China's National Defense, 2002, 2004, 2006, 2008, 2010; U.S. Department of Defense 2010 Annual Report to Congress on Military and Security Developments Involving the People's Republic of China; Indian Union Budget and Economic Survey: Expenditure Budget, 2000–2013; Japanese MoD White Papers, 2005–2011; South Korean MoD White Papers, 2000, 2006, 2008, 2010; South Korean MoD; Taiwanese National Defense Report, 2009 and 2011; analysis by CSIS Defense-Industrial Initiatives Group.

Growth in defense budgets for these five Asian countries over the last decade has not occurred in a linear manner. Instead, increases in defense spending visibly accelerated in the second half of the last decade. With the exception of South Korea, growth rates have been higher between 2005 and 2011 than between 2000 and 2005 (see Table 2). In the case of Taiwan, defense spending in fact decreased between 2000 and 2005, and then rose by a 4.3 percent CAGR between 2005 and 2011. These steeper growth trajectories in recent years might be a precursor for continued significant increases in defense spending, especially in light of large, high-profile investment decisions such as India's Medium Multi-Role Combat Aircraft (MMRCA) selection, Japan's F-35 order, or South Korea's F-X-3 multi-role fighter competition.

A comparative analysis of Asian defense spending must also take into account the exchange rates between local currencies and the U.S. dollar. For instance, the Japanese Yen gained 34.5 percent in value against the U.S. dollar between 2000 and 2011, and the Chinese Yuan increased in value against the U.S. dollar by 27.6 percent. As a consequence, changes in defense spending measured in constant 2011 U.S. dollars are inflated for some countries. Figure 1.3 below presents a cross-country comparison of indexed changes in total defense spending with 2000 as the base year, for the time period 2000–2011, in local currencies.

Figure 1.3. Indexed Total Defense Spending in Constant 2011 Local Currencies by Country (2000–2011)

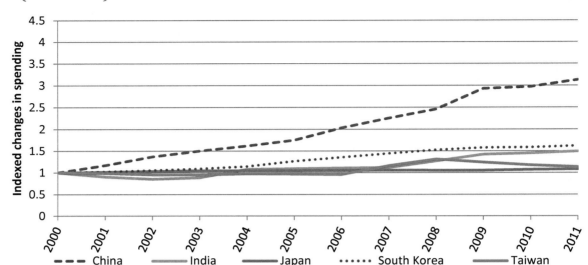

Sources: Chinese MoD White Papers, China's National Defense, 2002, 2004, 2006, 2008, 2010; U.S. Department of Defense 2010 Annual Report to Congress on Military and Security Developments Involving the People's Republic of China; Indian Union Budget and Economic Survey: Expenditure Budget, 2000–2013; Japanese MoD White Papers, 2005–2011; South Korean MoD White Papers, 2000, 2006, 2008, 2010; South Korean MoD; Taiwanese National Defense Report, 2009 and 2011; analysis by CSIS Defense-Industrial Initiatives Group.

A comparison of defense spending in U.S. dollars with spending in local currencies reveals the effect of exchange rate fluctuations. Measured in constant 2011 Yuan, the growth in China's defense budget still outpaces the rest of the group, yet with a CAGR of 10.9 percent (compared to 13.4 percent when measured in constant 2011 U.S. dollars). India's and South Korea's defense spending trends were the least affected by currency exchange fluctuations during the observed time period. Their respective 11-year CAGRs in constant 2011 local currency are 3.7 and 4.5 percent respectively in comparison to 3.6 and 4.8 percent when their defense spending is measured in constant 2011 U.S. dollars. Japan's and Taiwan's CAGRs for defense spending between 2000 and 2011 are both lower when measured in constant 2011 local currency, with a 0.7 percent and 1.1 percent CAGR, respectively (compared to 3.5 percent for Japan and 1.8 percent for Taiwan when measured in constant 2011 U.S. dollars).

The comparison of U.S. dollars versus local currency is also relevant when analyzing different categories of defense spending. In certain areas, such as Personnel costs, expenses are accrued in local currency. In others, such as acquisition expenditures, assessing trends in constant U.S. dollars might be more useful for countries that satisfy a considerable portion of their requirements through imports with dollar-based pricing. For these countries, fluctuations in exchange rates may significantly increase or decrease their buying power.

1.2   Defense Spending Per Soldier

Assessing defense spending on a per-soldier basis broadens the analytical prism and provides an additional perspective on topline defense trends. It captures the impact of changes to the force structure in conjunction with total defense spending trends. It can also be used as a proxy variable for the quality potential of armed forces as it measures the resources available for an individual soldier to be recruited, trained, compensated, equipped, and sustained.

Figure 1.4 depicts a cross-country comparison of per-soldier defense spending for the years 2000–2011.

Figure 1.4. Per-Soldier Defense Spending by Country (2000–2011)

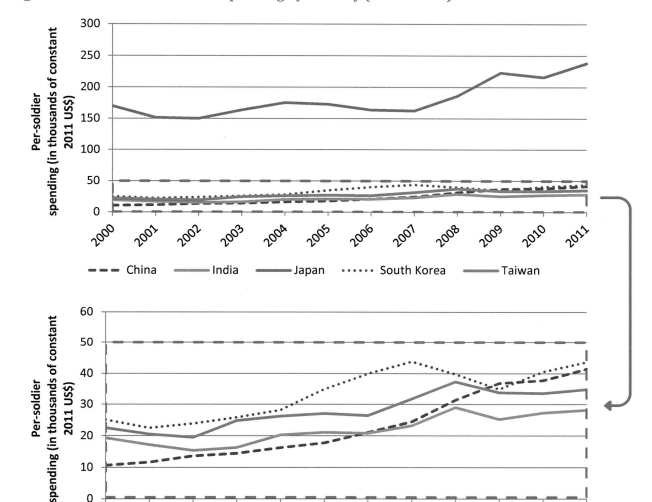

Sources: Chinese MoD White Papers, China's National Defense, 2002, 2004, 2006, 2008, 2010; U.S. Department of Defense 2010 Annual Report to Congress on Military and Security Developments Involving the People's Republic of China; Indian Union Budget and Economic Survey: Expenditure Budget, 2000–2013; Japanese MoD White Papers, 2005–2011; South Korean MoD White Papers, 2000, 2006, 2008, 2010; South Korean MoD; Taiwanese National Defense Report, 2009 and 2011; IISS Military Balance; analysis by CSIS Defense-Industrial Initiatives Group.

Analyzing defense spending on a per-soldier basis reveals a dramatic spending gap between Japan and the rest of the group. While the other four countries spent between $28,200 and $43,600 per service member in 2011, Japan allocated $238,100 per soldier in the same year (see Figure 1.4). This discrepancy was predominantly caused by the small size of the Japanese forces, approximately 244,300 troops in 2011, relative to the other countries. Troop levels in China, India, and South Korea were between 2.7 and 8.9 times higher than Japan's.

Although Taiwan had the smallest defense budget of the five countries analyzed (see Figure 1.1), the size of its military was comparable to that of Japan. As a result, Taiwan's per-soldier defense spending was similar to that of China, India, and South Korea, all of whom have to spread their larger defense budgets across a more personnel-heavy military.

Figure 1.5 provides a cross-country comparison of indexed changes in per-soldier defense spending, with 2000 as the base year, for the 2000–2011 timeframe.

Figure 1.5. Indexed Per-Soldier Defense Spending in Constant 2011 U.S. Dollars by Country (2000–2011)

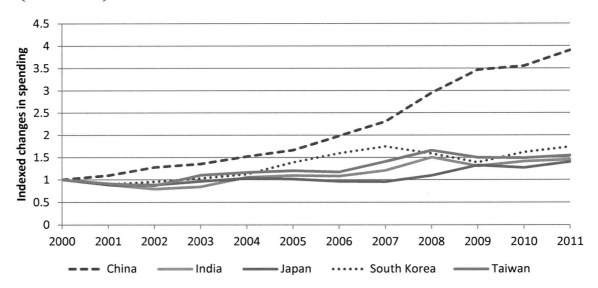

Sources: Chinese MoD White Papers, China's National Defense, 2002, 2004, 2006, 2008, 2010; U.S. Department of Defense 2010 Annual Report to Congress on Military and Security Developments Involving the People's Republic of China; Indian Union Budget and Economic Survey: Expenditure Budget, 2000–2013; Japanese MoD White Papers, 2005–2011; South Korean MoD White Papers, 2000, 2006, 2008, 2010; South Korean MoD; Taiwanese National Defense Report, 2009 and 2011; IISS Military Balance; analysis by CSIS Defense-Industrial Initiatives Group.

When measured in constant 2011 U.S. dollars, the spending trends on a per-soldier basis resemble the overall growth trends in total defense spending (see Figure 1.1). Three countries—China, Japan, and India—increased their troop numbers between 2000 and 2011, resulting in smaller growth rates in per-soldier spending when compared to their total defense spending (see Table 2). During the same period, South Korea and Taiwan reduced their troop levels, resulting in steeper growth trajectories in per-soldier defense spending than in total defense spending.

Table 2. CAGRs for Total and Per-Soldier Defense Spending in Constant 2011 U.S. Dollars by Country (2000–2011)

Countries	Defense Spending 2000–2011 CAGR	
	Total	**Per-Soldier**
China	13.4%	13.2%
India	3.6%	3.5%
Japan	3.5%	3.1%
South Korea	4.8%	5.2%
Taiwan	1.8%	4.0%

Sources: Chinese MoD White Papers, China's National Defense, 2002, 2004, 2006, 2008, 2010; U.S. Department of Defense 2010 Annual Report to Congress on Military and Security Developments Involving the People's Republic of China; Indian Union Budget and Economic Survey: Expenditure Budget, 2000–2013; Japanese MoD White Papers, 2005–2011; South Korean MoD White Papers, 2000, 2006, 2008, 2010; South Korean MoD; Taiwanese National Defense Report, 2009 and 2011; IISS Military Balance; analysis by CSIS Defense-Industrial Initiatives Group.

Overall, the deviations between the 11-year CAGRs for total and per-soldier defense spending are modest, due to relatively small fluctuations of troop levels in China, India, Japan, and South Korea. The major exception was Taiwan. A 21.6 percent reduction in troop numbers between 2000 and 2011 yielded a 4.0 percent CAGR for Taiwanese per-soldier defense spending, which represents a substantial increase over its 1.8 percent CAGR for total defense spending during the same timeframe. The impact of these force cuts was also illustrated by the fact that though Taiwan's overall defense spending grew the least among the countries analyzed in this report, its per-soldier spending grew at a faster pace than India's and Japan's.

2. Country Analysis

This section provides an in-depth country-by-country analysis of defense spending trends in five Asian countries: China, India, Japan, South Korea, and Taiwan. It discusses total and per-soldier spending trends and provides a breakdown of defense spending by functional categories: Defense Investment (which includes procurement, military construction, and R&D), Personnel, and O&M. For India, Japan, and South Korea, it breaks Defense Investment into Defense R&D and Defense Procurement.[3]

The charts in this section provide topline and per-soldier estimates for each country. Where available, they provide functional breakdowns of the defense budgets for individual countries, both in absolute terms and as percentage shares, across the years 2000–2011. In the case of China, both the official Chinese data and the SIPRI estimates are provided for topline estimates in addition to functional breakdowns from the Chinese government.

2.1 China

Figure 2.1. Total and Per-Soldier Defense Spending, China (2000–2010)

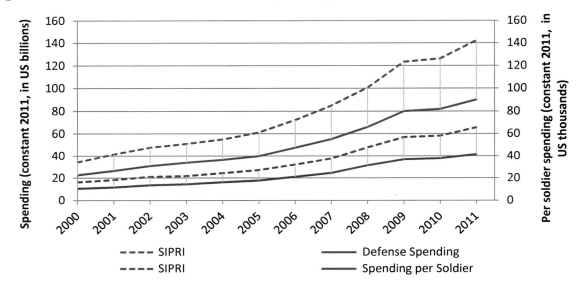

Sources: Chinese MoD White Papers, China's National Defense, 2002, 2004, 2006, 2008, 2010; U.S. Department of Defense 2010 Annual Report to Congress on Military and Security Developments Involving the People's Republic of China; IISS Military Balance; SIPRI Military Expenditure Database; analysis by CSIS Defense-Industrial Initiatives Group.

Total defense (left-side y-axis) and per-soldier spending (right-side y-axis) as reported by China are significantly lower than the third-party estimates by the Stockholm International Peace Research

---

[3] The Methodology section provides a detailed explanation for the definitions and compositions of the individual defense spending categories. It should be noted that not all countries provide sufficient details in their budget documents to allow for a breakdown into each of the categories assessed in this report. For instance, the analysis of R&D spending only covers India, Japan, and South Korea. For China, detailed budget breakdowns are not available for all years between 2000 and 2011, and 2009 is the most recent year for which a detailed budget breakdown is available.

Institute (SIPRI) (see Figure 2.1).[4] As a result of this large discrepancy, CSIS analyzed total and per-soldier spending according to both sources to depict the possible range of China's total defense expenditure.

Data provided by China indicate spending in 2000 of roughly $22.5 billion in constant 2011 U.S. dollars. Increasing at an 11-year CAGR of 13.4 percent, defense spending peaked at $89.9 billion in 2011. SIPRI values China's total defense spending at around $34.2 billion in 2000, increasing annually until its highest total of $142.2 billion in 2011 (11-year CAGR of 13.8 percent). The gap between official Chinese data and SIPRI estimates ranges from $11.7 billion (2000) to $52.3 billion (2011). However, official Chinese and SIPRI estimates of total defense spending differ only slightly with regard to growth trajectories, as indicated by their 11-year CAGRs, which vary by less than 0.5 percent.

According to both SIPRI and Chinese data, per-soldier spending also increased at near identical 11-year CAGRs of 13.6 percent (SIPRI) and 13.2 percent (official Chinese data). However, as was the case with total defense expenditures, there was a gap in absolute terms between SIPRI estimates and official Chinese data, which ranged from $5,500 per soldier (2000) to $23,100 per soldier (2011).

Figure 2.2 Total Defense Spending by Category, China (2000–2010)

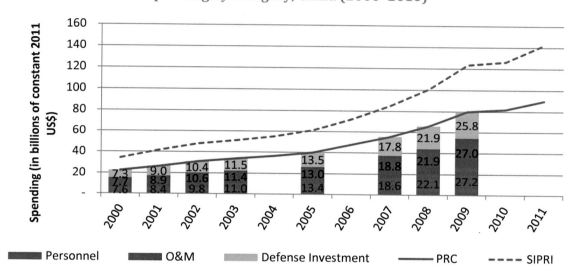

Note: 2008 breakdown data were provided by China to the United Nations and republished in the U.S. Department of Defense 2010 Annual Report to Congress on Military and Security Developments Involving the People's Republic of China.

Sources: Chinese MoD White Papers, China's National Defense, 2002, 2004, 2006, 2008, 2010; U.S. Department of Defense 2010 Annual Report to Congress on Military and Security Developments Involving the People's Republic of China; SIPRI Military Expenditure Database; analysis by CSIS Defense-Industrial Initiatives Group.

Figure 2.2 above reflects the breakdown of official defense spending data provided by China (see Figure 2.1). Although topline data are available for all years, a category breakdown is not available for years 2004, 2006, 2010, and 2011. The spending categories include Personnel, O&M, and Defense Investment, which combines procurement, military construction, and R&D.

---

[4] SIPRI only provides total defense spending estimates. SIPRI per-soldier spending is calculated based on SIPRI total defense spending estimates.

Instantly noticeable is the near equal share (in absolute terms) of total dollars spent across all three categories. During the early years especially (2000 to 2005), spending per category varied, relative to each other, by less than $800 million. Ultimately, Chinese values for Personnel, O&M, and Defense Investment all increased from a $7.3–$7.7 billion range in 2000 to a $25.8–$27.2 billion range in 2009, at 15.3, 14.9, and 15.1 percent CAGRS, respectively.

Due to the similar growth patterns of Chinese and SIPRI data, CSIS utilized the official percentage breakdowns of the defense categories as provided by China to generate approximate values using SIPRI topline estimates. As a result, 9-year CAGRs are identical to official Chinese breakdowns, but differences arose in absolute terms. Specifically, values derived from SIPRI topline estimates indicated spending levels with an $11.0–$11.7 billion range per category in 2000. By 2009, this range was between $18.3 and $19.3 billion (see Figure 2.1).

Figure 2.3. Distribution of Total Defense Spending by Category, China (2000–2010)

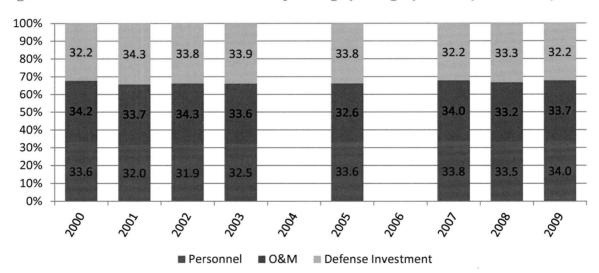

Note: 2008 breakdown data were provided by China to the United Nations and republished in the U.S. Department of Defense 2010 Annual Report to Congress on Military and Security Developments Involving the People's Republic of China.

Sources: Chinese MoD White Papers, China's National Defense, 2002, 2004, 2006, 2008, 2010; U.S. Department of Defense 2010 Annual Report to Congress on Military and Security Developments Involving the People's Republic of China; SIPRI Military Expenditure Database; analysis by CSIS Defense-Industrial Initiatives Group.

The symmetry of Chinese allocations to individual defense spending categories is particularly noticeable when broken down by each category's share of total defense spending. As reflected in Figure 2.3, each category claimed approximately one-third of total spending, with only slight annual variations. Despite a minor dip from 2001 to 2003, Personnel hovered at around 33 percent before rising slightly to 34.0 percent in 2009. O&M's share also fluctuated between 33 and 34 percent for all years except in 2005, when it fell slightly to 32.6 percent, and Defense Investment spending varied between 32 and nearly 34 percent, with zero percentage change between 2000 and 2009.

Figure 2.4. Per-Soldier Defense Spending by Category, China (2000–2010)

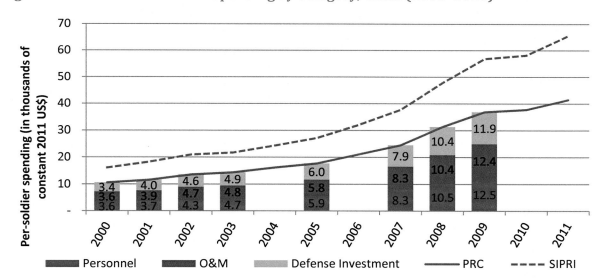

Note: 2008 breakdown data were provided by China to the United Nations and republished in the U.S. Department of Defense 2010 Annual Report to Congress on Military and Security Developments Involving the People's Republic of China.

Sources: Chinese MoD White Papers, China's National Defense, 2002, 2004, 2006, 2008, 2010; U.S. Department of Defense 2010 Annual Report to Congress on Military and Security Developments Involving the People's Republic of China; IISS Military Balance; SIPRI Military Expenditure Database; analysis by CSIS Defense-Industrial Initiatives Group.

In absolute terms, per-soldier spending for each category increased from roughly $3,500 in 2000 to just below $5,000 in 2003. Beginning in 2005, however, annual growth accelerated, increasing from between $5,800 and $6,000 in 2005 to between $11,900 and $12,500 in 2009. Overall, Personnel, O&M, and Defense Investment per-soldier spending increased at 15.0, 14.9, and 14.6 percent CAGRs respectively between 2000 and 2009.

SIPRI per-soldier spending per category again reflects relatively higher estimates. Specifically, in 2000, SIPRI estimates per category hovered at just over $5,000 and increased to $18,000 and $19,000 by 2009.

Summary

China's total defense spending and per-soldier spending increased considerably in the years 2000 to 2010. Official Chinese data estimated total defense spending to have increased from $22.5 to $89.9 billion between 2000 and 2011; however, SIPRI estimates ranged from $34.2 to $142.2 billion. While official Chinese sources reflect a total growth of almost 300 percent between 2000 and 2011, SIPRI reflects a slightly higher growth estimate of approximately 315 percent. 11-year CAGRs for official Chinese estimates and SIPRI are 13.4 and 13.8 percent, respectively. Similarly, per-soldier spending derived from SIPRI topline estimates was approximately $5,500 higher in 2000 than the value provided by official Chinese sources. This gap gradually widened to a difference of $23,100 in 2011. In other terms, Chinese total defense spending and per-soldier spending accounted for between 63.2 and 65.9 percent of SIPRI estimates for all years. Broken down by defense spending categories using official Chinese data, total and per-soldier spending on Personnel, O&M, and Defense Investment each claimed roughly one-third of total defense spending for the entire time period.

2.2 India

Figure 2.5. Total and Per-Soldier Defense Spending, India (2000–2011)

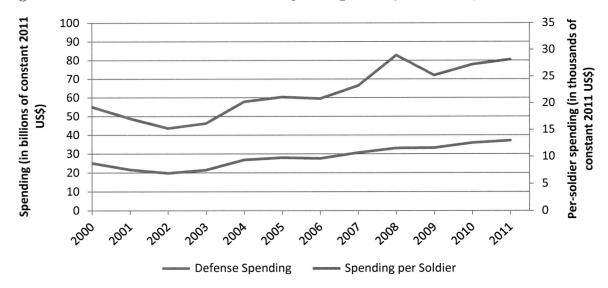

Sources: Indian Union Budget and Economic Survey: Expenditure Budget, 2000–2013; IISS Military Balance; analysis by CSIS Defense-Industrial Initiatives Group.

For the years 2000 to 2011, India's total defense spending (left-side y-axis) and total defense spending per soldier (right-side y-axis) increased at similar 11-year CAGRs of 3.6 and 3.5 percent. Defense spending fell from $25.1 billion in 2000 to its lowest point of $19.8 billion in 2002 before steadily growing to reach a record $37.0 billion in 2011. Relative to total defense spending, per-soldier spending showed greater fluctuation. From around $19,300 in 2000, it increased to $28,200 by 2011. The variance in per-soldier spending is largely attributable to changes in force structure in 2000–2011, while total defense spending rose steadily.

Figure 2.6. Total Defense Spending by Category, India (2000–2011)

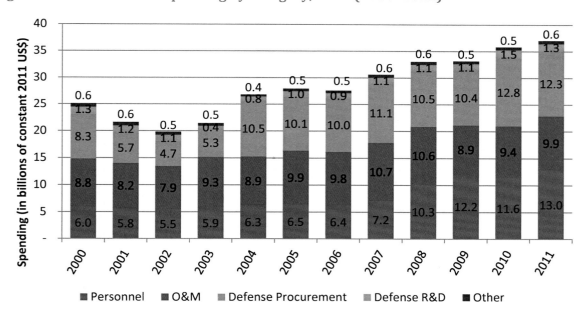

Sources: Indian Union Budget and Economic Survey: Expenditure Budget, 2000–2013; analysis by CSIS Defense-Industrial Initiatives Group.

The largest category in terms of dollars spent in 2011 was Personnel, which grew from $6.0 billion in 2000 to $13.0 billion in 2011. Relative to the other categories, when analyzed by total percentage growth, spending on Personnel also averaged the largest 11-year CAGR (7.2 percent). Increasing at a slower rate during the years 2000–2007, Personnel grew dramatically between 2007 and 2011. This is noteworthy given that during the 11-year timeframe, total troop numbers increased by less than 1 percent.

India's Defense Procurement spending grew from $8.3 billion in 2000 to $12.3 billion in 2011 (an 11-year CAGR of 3.6 percent). Much of this growth can be attributed to India's modernization of its armed forces, which until the late 1990s, was still largely reliant on Soviet-era technology and equipment. The Indian Air Force has been particularly active in the past decade, increasing its share of capital spending with the purchase of new aircraft, sensors, radars, satellites, and unmanned aerial vehicles (UAVs).[5]

Spending on O&M increased more modestly than Defense Procurement and Personnel, from $8.8 billion in 2000 to $9.9 billion in 2011 (an 11-year CAGR of 1.1 percent). The greatest spending ($10.7 and $10.6 billion) occurred in 2007 and 2008, and although O&M decreased to $8.9 billion the following year, it grew by more than $500 million in both 2010 and 2011.

Despite a steady 47.6 percent increase in India's total defense spending during the 2000–2011 timeframe, Defense R&D fluctuated greatly with a low of $400 million in 2003 and a high of $1.5 billion in 2010. Dollars spent on the "Other" category decreased from $645 million in 2000 to $575 million in 2011.

---

[5] For more on India's defense modernization, see S. Amer Latif, *U.S.-India Defense Trade: Opportunities for Deepening the Partnership* (Washington, DC: CSIS, June 2012), pp. 10–11, http://csis.org/files/publication/ 120703_Latif_USIndiaDefense_Web.pdf.

Figure 2.7. Distribution of Total Defense Spending by Category, India (2000–2011)

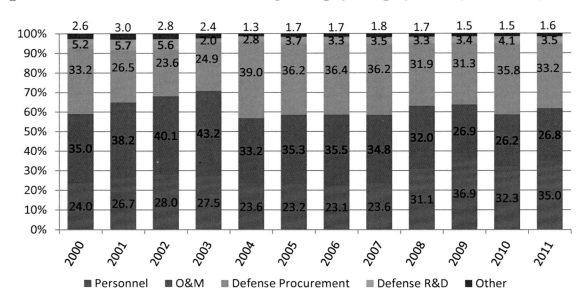

Sources: Indian Union Budget and Economic Survey: Expenditure Budget, 2000–2013; analysis by CSIS Defense-Industrial Initiatives Group.

For the period 2000–2011, there are three fairly distinct phases in the distribution of India's defense budget. Notably, the first phase, 2000–2003, showed an increase in Personnel from 24.0 to 27.5 percent, as well as a jump in O&M spending from 35.0 to 43.2 percent. However, Defense Procurement during this period decreased from roughly one-third of total spending to less than one-quarter. During 2000–2002, Defense R&D spending was held steady at around 5.5 percent before dropping sharply to 2.0 percent in 2003. Meanwhile, spending on "Other" hovered between 2.4 and 3.0 percent up until 2003.

The second phase spans from 2004–2007. During this phase, spending on Personnel remained virtually stable at its low of around 23 percent, as did O&M in the mid-30 percent range. Despite drastically increasing in 2004 to 39.0 percent, Defense Procurement restabilized at around 36 percent through 2007. In absolute terms, the 2004 jump in percentage share equates to an increase of more than $5 billion in Defense Procurement spending.

The third phase, in the years 2008–2011, showed a relative increase for Personnel spending, accounting for between 31.1 percent of total defense spending in 2008 and 36.9 percent in 2009. At the same time, O&M decreased significantly from 32.0 percent in 2008 to around 26 percent for the years 2009 to 2011. Defense Procurement spending initially declined down to 31.3 percent in 2009, but rebounded afterward and was allocated at 33.2 percent of overall defense spending in 2011.

Figure 2.8. Per-Soldier Defense Spending by Category, India (2000-2011)

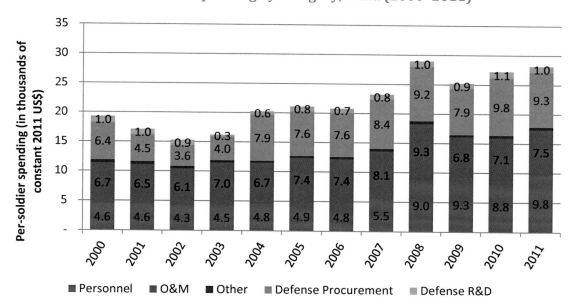

Sources: Indian Union Budget and Economic Survey: Expenditure Budget, 2000–2013; IISS Military Balance; analysis by CSIS Defense-Industrial Initiatives Group.

Of the four categories, Personnel and Defense Procurement incurred the largest increases in per-soldier spending during the 12-year time period. Although largely stable between 2000 and 2006, per-soldier spending on Personnel nearly doubled to approximately $9,000 in 2008, where it remained through 2011, peaking at $9,800. This resulted in an 11-year CAGR of 7.1 percent and a 6-year CAGR (2005–2011) of 12.3 percent. The strong growth in 2008 can largely be explained by the $3 billion jump in total Personnel expenditure in that year, coupled with a decrease in troop levels.

Defense Procurement spending per soldier grew a total of 46.0 percent between 2000 and 2011 (an 11-year CAGR of 3.5 percent). Roughly $6,400 in 2000, Defense Procurement spending per soldier subsequently fell to a low of $3,600 in 2002. However, in the subsequent years, spending grew significantly, reaching its peak of $9,800 in 2010. This spending trend mirrored that of total Defense Procurement spending for the same time period.

Per-soldier spending on O&M experienced slower growth between 2000 and 2011 with an 11-year CAGR of 1.0 percent. However, in 2007 and 2008 there was higher than normal spending of $8,100 and $9,300, respectively. This is largely due to India's total O&M spending of roughly $10.6 billion for these years and a simultaneous decrease in its force structure.

Despite decreased spending on Defense R&D between 2003 and 2007, per-soldier spending on R&D ranged between $900 and $1,100 for 2008–2011. Meanwhile, the "Other" category remained at less than $500 per soldier each year.

Summary

India's total defense budget and per-soldier spending followed similar growth trajectories for all years except 2008, increasing at 11-year CAGRs of 3.6 and 3.5 percent, respectively (see Figure 2.5). Despite dropping slightly between 2001 and 2004, total defense and per-soldier spending resumed an upward trend the following year. Analyzed by defense spending categories, spending on Personnel accounted for the largest share of total defense dollars and also experienced the most significant growth in absolute terms during the same time period.

2.3 Japan

Figure 2.9. Total and Per-Soldier Defense Spending, Japan (2000–2011)

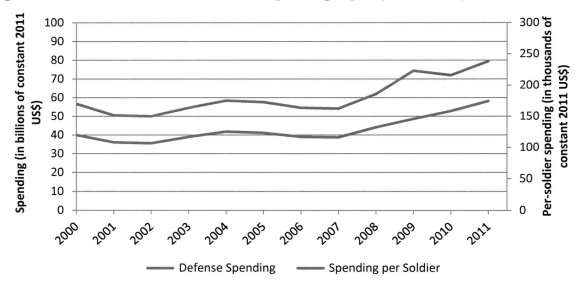

Sources: Japanese MoD White Papers, 2005–2011; IISS Military Balance; analysis by CSIS Defense-Industrial Initiatives Group.

Japan boasts the second-largest total defense spending of the countries examined in this report and the largest spending per soldier by a large margin.[6] Total defense spending (left side y-axis in Chart 14 above) increased in absolute terms from $40.0 billion in 2000 to $58.2 billion in 2011 (an 11-year CAGR of 3.5 percent). With annual fluctuations ranging between -9.9 and 9.4 percent for the period 2000–2007, defense spending began a steady upward trend in 2008 with strong growth of 13.8 percent followed by year-on-year increases of approximately 10 percent.

Following a near identical growth trajectory, spending per soldier (right side y-axis) also fluctuated annually between 2000 and 2007, ranging between a low of $149,900 and a high of $175,300 per soldier. In 2008, spending grew by 14.5 percent to reach $185,800 per soldier, after which it increased by 21.3 percent in 2009 and 10.3 percent in 2011, peaking at $238,100.

---

[6] The annual defense expenditures reported in the Japanese Ministry of Defense White Papers include expenditures for U.S. forces stationed in Japan, but exclude expenditures related to the Special Action Committee on Okinawa as well as U.S. force realignment expenditures.

Figure 2.10. Total Defense Spending by Category, Japan (2000–2011)

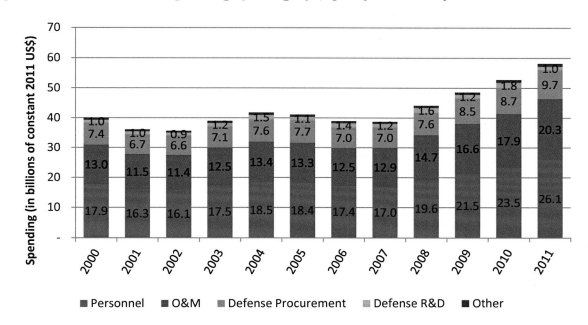

Sources: Japanese MoD White Papers, 2005–2011; analysis by CSIS Defense-Industrial Initiatives Group.

In the years 2000 to 2007, spending for Personnel ranged between a low of $16.1 billion and a high of $18.5 billion. The greatest growth occurred in 2008, when total spending reached $19.6 billion. Ultimately, between 2000 and 2011, total dollars spent on this category increased at an 11-year CAGR of 3.5 percent. Despite growth in absolute terms, relative to the other categories and as a share of overall spending, costs associated with Personnel remained fairly constant (see Figure 2.10).

In absolute terms, O&M increased from $13.0 billion in 2000 to $20.3 billion in 2011, a total increase of 55.7 percent (an 11-year CAGR of 4.1 percent). Similar to spending on Personnel, O&M fluctuated only marginally between 2000 and 2007, before experiencing year-on-year growth beginning in 2008.

Unlike Personnel and O&M, dollars spent on Defense Procurement accounted for less than 20 percent of total defense spending, with only $7.4 billion in 2000 and $9.7 billion in 2011 (see Figure 2.10). Fluctuating by less than $3.1 billion across all years examined, Defense Procurement increased at an 11-year CAGR of 2.5 percent.

Figure 2.11. Distribution of Total Spending Defense Spending by Category, Japan (2000–2011)

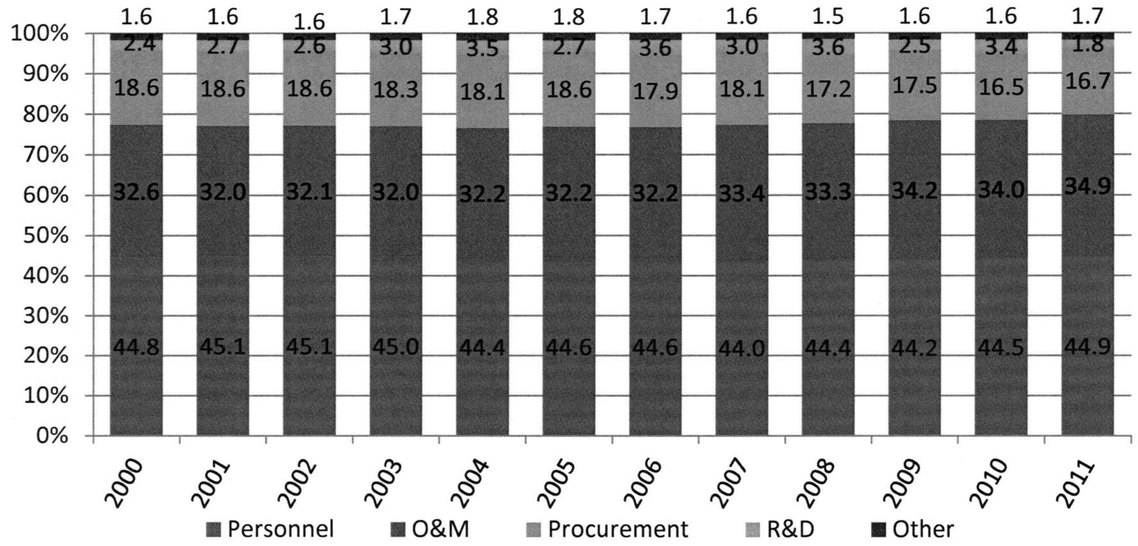

	2000	2001	2002	2003	2004	2005	2006	2007	2008	2009	2010	2011
Other	1.6	1.6	1.6	1.7	1.8	1.8	1.7	1.6	1.5	1.6	1.6	1.7
R&D	2.4	2.7	2.6	3.0	3.5	2.7	3.6	3.0	3.6	2.5	3.4	1.8
Procurement	18.6	18.6	18.6	18.3	18.1	18.6	17.9	18.1	17.2	17.5	16.5	16.7
O&M	32.6	32.0	32.1	32.0	32.2	32.2	32.2	33.4	33.3	34.2	34.0	34.9
Personnel	44.8	45.1	45.1	45.0	44.4	44.6	44.6	44.0	44.4	44.2	44.5	44.9

■ Personnel ■ O&M ■ Procurement ▨ R&D ■ Other

Sources: Japanese MoD White Papers, 2005–2011; analysis by CSIS Defense-Industrial Initiatives Group.

Analyzing defense expenditure by each category's share of total defense spending reveals that the largest category, Personnel, claimed a share of 44.8 percent in 2000 and remained essentially unchanged at 44.9 percent in 2011 with annual fluctuations of less than 1 percent. O&M showed slightly more variation over the 2000–2011 timeframe: between 2000 and 2006, its share of overall defense spending remained constant at around 32 percent, then grew to 34.9 percent in 2011. This increase was largely the result of a sharp decrease for Defense R&D to 1.8 percent in 2011, down from its previous 2.4 to 3.6 percent range. Similar to R&D, the share of Defense Procurement also decreased from 18.6 percent in 2000 to 16.7 percent in 2011.This decrease suggests that relative to Personnel and O&M, dollars for Defense Procurement are not increasing at the same or constant rate. In terms of the share of the total defense budget allocated to Defense Procurement, Defense R&D, and Defense Investment (the combination of procurement and R&D), Japan ranks last among the five countries analyzed. The remaining four countries all spent about 30 to 35 percent of their defense budgets on Defense Investment.

Figure 2.12. Per-Soldier Defense Spending by Category, Japan (2000–2011)

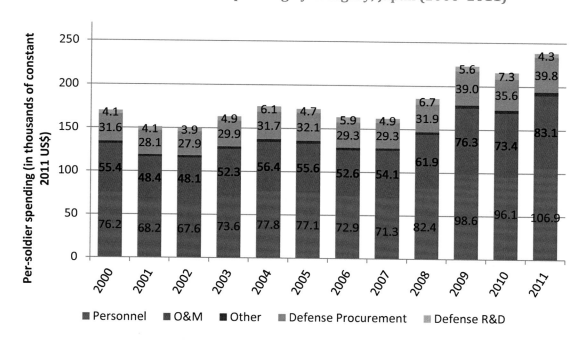

Sources: Japanese MoD White Papers, 2005–2011; IISS Military Balance; analysis by CSIS Defense-Industrial Initiatives Group.

Japan's per-soldier defense spending far exceeded that of any of the other four Asian countries examined in this report, ranging from $170,000 in 2000 to a record $238,100 in 2011. For all years, the largest share of the budget was spent on Personnel, which relative to the other categories, maintained a share of approximately 44 to 45 percent, equal to between $68,200 and $106,900 spent per soldier.

O&M spending per soldier fluctuated moderately between 2000 and 2007 (ranging from a low of $48,100 to a high of $56,400) before increasing to above $70,000 as of 2009 and peaking at $83,100 in 2011. Analyzed by percentage share, O&M spending per soldier consistently accounted for about one-third of spending.

In absolute terms, Defense Procurement spending per soldier grew from $31,600 in 2000 to $39,800 in 2011 at an 11-year CAGR of 2.1 percent. As a share of total defense dollars, this equated to between 16.5 percent (2010) and 18.6 percent (2000).

Per-solider spending on Defense R&D increased only slightly from $4,100 in 2000 to $4,300 in 2011 at an 11-year CAGR of 0.5 percent. Despite this relative stability, spending reached as high as $6,700 and $7,300 per soldier in 2008 and 2010, respectively. Spending on "Other" ranged between $2,400 and $4,000 for all years.

Summary

As illustrated in Figure 2.9, per-soldier spending largely mirrored increases in total defense spending. Specifically, total defense and per-soldier spending increased at 11-year CAGRs of 3.5 and 3.1 percent, respectively. Broken down by defense spending categories (see Figure 2.10), Personnel accounted for the majority of defense dollars spent. Relative to the spending increases of more than $7 billion in Personnel and O&M between 2000 and 2011, Defense Procurement grew by a more modest $2.3 billion. Spending on Defense R&D was a small fraction of total defense spending and increased by 9.1 percent between 2000 and 2011. Analyzed by percentage share of total defense spending (see Figure 2.11), Personnel spending remained nearly constant for all years, whereas O&M experienced growth, and Defense Procurement and Defense R&D both declined.

2.4   South Korea

Figure 2.13. Total and Per-Soldier Defense Spending, South Korea (2000–2011)

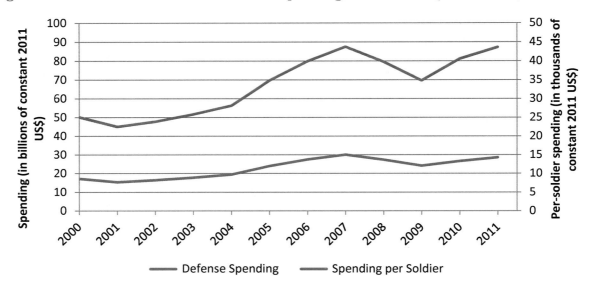

Sources: South Korean MoD White Papers, 2000, 2006, 2008, 2010; South Korean MoD; IISS Military Balance; analysis by CSIS Defense-Industrial Initiatives Group.

South Korea's total defense spending increased in constant 2011 dollars from $17.1 billion in 2000 to $28.6 billion in 2011, equating to a 4.8 percent CAGR (see Figure 2.13).[7] However, this growth did not unfold in a linear manner. In fact, South Korea experienced declines in defense spending between 2000 and 2001 and again between 2007 and 2009. The most significant growth took place between 2005 and 2007 leading to a spending peak of $30.1 billion in 2007.

Trends in defense spending on a per-soldier basis largely mirrored developments in total defense spending as South Korea's force structure remained stable during this time. With the exception of 2009, South Korea boasted the second-largest per-soldier spending of all five countries examined. Per-soldier spending increased from around $25,100 in 2000 to $43,600 in 2011, with peak spending of $43,700 in 2007, commensurate to the jump in total defense spending in the same year.

---

[7] The annual defense expenditures reported by the government of the Republic of Korea Ministry of National Defense in its annual Defense White Papers include costs for relocating U.S. forces in Korea under the O&M category.

Figure 2.14. Total Defense Spending by Category, South Korea (2000–2011)

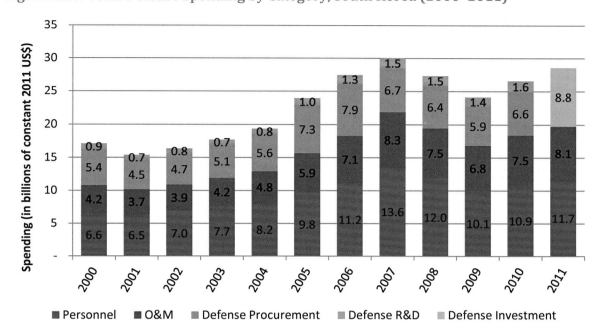

Sources: South Korean MoD White Papers, 2000, 2006, 2008, 2010; South Korean MoD; analysis by CSIS Defense-Industrial Initiatives Group.

Absolute trends in the individual defense spending categories largely paralleled developments in the overall defense budgets. The majority of South Korea's defense spending was allocated to Personnel, which accounted for approximately $6.6 billion in 2000 (see Figure 2.14). Increasing at a 5.4 percent CAGR, it nearly doubled to $11.7 billion in 2011, peaking in 2007 with $13.6 billion.

Spending on O&M nearly doubled from roughly $4.2 billion in 2000 to $8.1 billion in 2011 (6.1 percent CAGR). In 2007, spending on O&M replaced Defense Procurement spending as the second-largest defense spending category with a total of $8.3 billion. Following a growth pattern similar to total defense spending, O&M went through a period of noticeably stronger growth beginning in 2005.

Defense Procurement spending remained relatively stable between 2000 and 2004, ranging between a low of $4.5 and a high of $5.6 billion. Starting in 2005, it expanded substantially reaching $7.3 and $7.9 billion in 2005 and 2006, respectively, before dropping to the $5.9 to $6.7 billion range during 2008 to 2010. Defense R&D spending grew from $0.9 billion in 2000 to $1.6 billion in 2010, equating to a 10-year CAGR of 6.3 percent. Note that in Figure 2.14, Defense Investment spending is provided for 2011 in lieu of Defense Procurement and Defense R&D spending. Defense Investment spending combines the totals for Defense Procurement and Defense R&D, as a detailed breakdown of South Korea's expenditure for these categories was not available for 2011. However, the 2011 value of $8.8 billion for Defense Investment is suggestive of continued positive growth for Defense Procurement and Defense R&D spending, as both categories combined accounted for a total of $8.2 billion the previous year.

Figure 2.15. Distribution of Total Defense Spending by Category, South Korea (2000–2011)

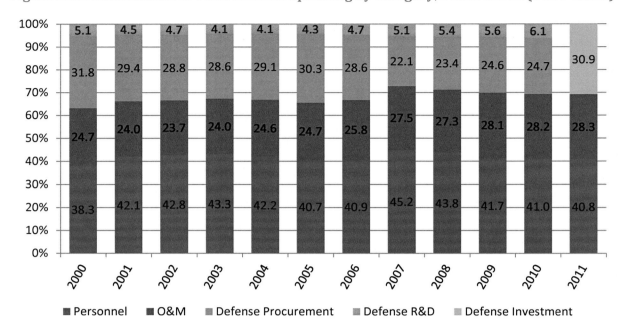

Sources: South Korean MoD White Papers, 2000, 2006, 2008, 2010; South Korean MoD; analysis by CSIS Defense-Industrial Initiatives Group.

The distribution of South Korea's total defense spending shows that Personnel spending accounted for over 40 percent for all years except 2000. Its largest share of 45.2 percent in 2007 coincides with the sharp increase in total spending in the same year. In the years 2008–2011, the share of Personnel spending decreased annually, eventually dropping to 40.8 percent.

O&M accounted for a low of 23.7 and a high of 24.7 percent of defense spending between 2000 and 2005. After 2005, its relative share began to increase, reaching 28.3 percent in 2011. Defense Procurement spending ranged between 31.8 and 28.6 percent during 2000 and 2006. It then contracted considerably in 2007, reaching a low of 22.1 percent, and subsequently increased to a 24.7 percent share of defense spending in 2010.

Relative to India and Japan, the other two countries for which Defense R&D data are available, South Korea's Defense R&D accounted for a considerably larger share of its total defense spending. Despite experiencing relative declines in the early 2000s, it increased from 5.1 percent in 2000 to 6.1 percent in 2010.

Figure 2.16. Per-Soldier Defense Spending by Category, South Korea (2000–2011)

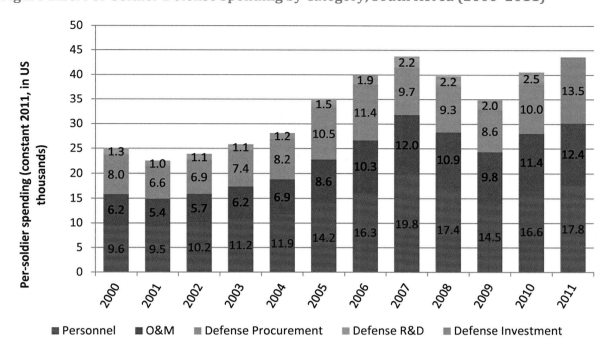

Sources: South Korean MoD White Papers, 2000, 2006, 2008, 2010; South Korean MoD; IISS Military Balance; analysis by CSIS Defense-Industrial Initiatives Group.

Broken down by category, growth patterns for per-soldier spending largely mirror those of total defense spending due to South Korea's stable force structure. Specifically, spending on Personnel in 2011 constant dollars represented the largest defense spending category for all years, nearly doubling over the 11-year time frame from $9,600 to $17,800 (5.8 percent CAGR). Personnel spending peaked in 2007 with a total of $19,800, paralleling developments in total defense spending.

O&M per-soldier spending outpaced all other defense spending categories with a 6.5 percent 11-year CAGR, growing from $6,200 to $12,400 between 2000 and 2011. Defense Procurement spending per-soldier increased from $8,000 to $10,000 between 2000 and 2010 (2.3 percent 10-year CAGR). Per-soldier spending on Defense R&D nearly doubled from $1,300 to $2,500 in the same timeframe and experienced the greatest jump in absolute terms in 2009 to 2010.

Summary

South Korea's total defense spending increased from $17.1 in 2000 to its peak of $30.1 billion in 2007. By 2011, total defense spending was $28.6 billion (11-year CAGR of 4.8 percent). Per-soldier spending increased in a similar manner growing from $25,100 in 2000 to $43,600 in 2011 (an 11-year CAGR of 5.2 percent). This symmetry between total and per-soldier defense spending was the result of South Korea maintaining a relatively stable force structure between 2000 and 2011. Personnel was the largest spending category, nearly doubling in absolute terms between 2000 and 2011 (5.4 percent CAGR). Spending on O&M increased at the highest pace with a CAGR of 6.1 percent. Meanwhile, Defense Procurement and R&D, which in 2011 combined to form the second-largest category in absolute terms, experienced relatively slow growth with 10-year CAGRs of 1.9 and 6.3 respectively.

2.5 Taiwan

Figure 2.17. Total and Per-Soldier Defense Spending, Taiwan (2000–2011)

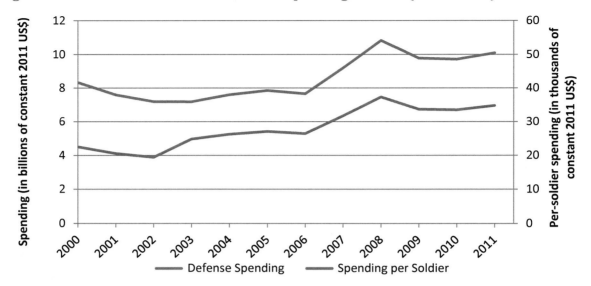

Sources: Taiwanese National Defense Report, 2009 and 2011; IISS Military Balance; analysis by CSIS Defense-Industrial Initiatives Group.

Taiwan's total defense spending grew from $8.3 billion in 2000 to $10.1 billion in 2011. Despite experiencing a slight decrease from 2001 to 2003, in the years that followed it resumed an upward growth trend peaking in 2008 with spending of $10.8 billion. Overall, total defense spending grew at an 11-year CAGR of 1.8 percent.

Per-soldier spending increased in a similar fashion, growing in absolute terms from $22,500 in 2000 to $34,800 in 2011. Relative to total defense spending, spending per soldier increased more quickly at a 4.0 percent 11-year CAGR. The decrease in Taiwan's force structure from roughly 370,000 to 290,000 caused this difference between total and per-soldier spending trends. Like total defense spending, per-soldier spending peaked in 2008 at $37,300, which was the direct result of a 17.7 percent increase in total defense spending in that year.

Figure 2.18. Total Defense Spending by Category, Taiwan (2000–2011)

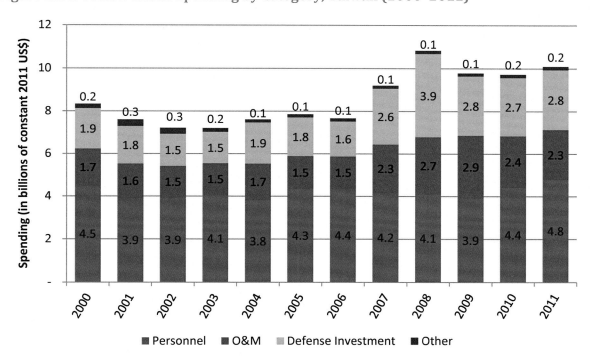

Sources: Taiwanese National Defense Report, 2009 and 2011; analysis by CSIS Defense-Industrial Initiatives Group.

Taiwan's spending on Personnel was the highest in 2000 and 2011 with $4.5 billion and $4.8 billion, respectively (an 11-year CAGR of 0.6 percent). In all other years, spending fluctuated between $3.8 and $4.4 billion. It is noteworthy that Taiwan allocated identical amounts of $4.1 billion to Personnel spending in the year of its lowest and highest total defense budgets (2003 and 2008). Spending on O&M increased from $1.7 to $2.3 billion between 2000 and 2011, respectively (CAGR of 2.8 percent). The largest increase in absolute terms occurred in 2007 with spending of $2.3 billion, up from $1.5 billion in the previous year. This upward growth continued with peak spending of $2.9 billion in 2009 after which spending decreased annually to $2.3 billion in 2011.

Increasing at a 3.6 percent CAGR, Defense Investment spending increased from $1.9 billion in 2000 to $2.8 billion in 2011. Paralleling the fluctuations in Taiwan's total defense spending, Defense Investment spending was at its lowest in 2003 ($1.5 billion) and at its highest in 2008 ($3.9 billion).

Figure 2.19. Distribution of Total Defense Spending by Category, Taiwan (2000–2009)

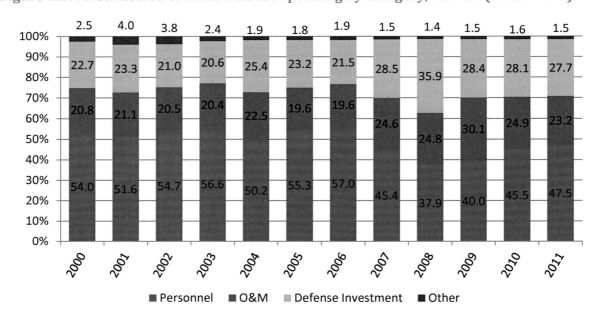

Sources: Taiwanese National Defense Report, 2009 and 2011; analysis by CSIS Defense-Industrial Initiatives Group.

Taiwan's defense budget was very Personnel heavy, with that category accounting for at least a 50 percent share of total spending until 2006. In the subsequent years, Personnel spending ranged between a low of 37.9 percent (2008) and a high of 47.5 percent (2011).

O&M spending share grew significantly in the 2007 to 2011 timeframe, having been relatively stable between 19.6 to 22.5 percent during the 2000–2006 timeframe. It reached its relative peak of 30.1 percent in 2009 and held a share of 23.2 percent in 2011.

With the exception of 2009, Defense Investment spending constituted the second-largest defense spending category, claiming between 20.6 and 25.4 percent for the 2000–2006 period. By 2008, Defense Investment reached 35.9 percent. Its share then progressively declined to 27.7 in 2011.

Figure 2.20. Per-Soldier Defense Spending, Taiwan (2000–2009)

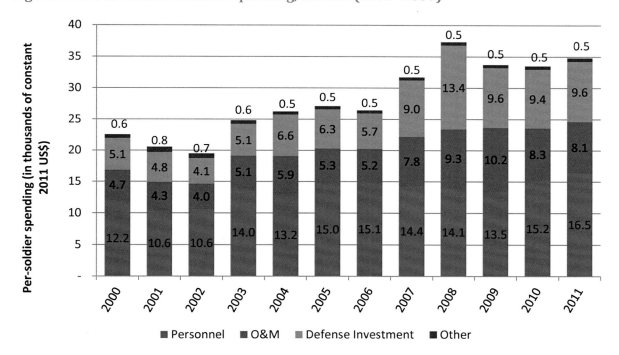

Sources: Taiwanese National Defense Report, 2009 and 2011; IISS Military Balance; analysis by CSIS Defense-Industrial Initiatives Group.

Personnel per-soldier spending constituted the largest per-soldier spending category. It grew in absolute terms from $12,200 to $16,500 between 2000 and 2011 at a CAGR of 2.8 percent, constituting the flattest growth trajectory of all the three major spending categories.

O&M spending per soldier increased from $4,700 to $8,100 between 2000 and 2011 (CAGR of 5.1 percent). It peaked in 2008 and 2009 with spending of $9,300 and $10,200, respectively, before dropping to just above $8,000 for the remaining two years.

Per-soldier spending on Defense Investment incurred the greatest growth in absolute terms, increasing from $5,100 in 2000 to $9,600 in 2011 (5.9 percent CAGR). Consistent with total defense spending patterns, Defense Investment spending per soldier peaked in 2008 at $13,400 but has since remained around $9,600. The spike in 2008 was the result of a near $1.3 billion increase in total Defense Investment spending in that year as total troop numbers remained constant.

Summary

Of all countries analyzed in this report, Taiwan has the smallest defense budget, which grew from $8.3 billion in 2000 to $10.1 billion in 2011 (CAGR of 1.8 percent). The strong growth in total defense spending from 2007 onward was largely the result of increased spending on Defense Investment and O&M, though Personnel remains the largest category. Per-soldier spending grew at a faster pace (4.0 percent CAGR), largely a result of significant troop reductions.

3. Defense Spending Categories

This section provides an in-depth analysis of the defense spending trends in the five countries by breaking down budgets into functional defense spending categories: Defense Investment (which includes procurement, military construction, and R&D), Personnel, O&M, and Defense R&D (for India, Japan, and South Korea only).[8]

3.1   Defense Investment

Figure 3.1 provides a country-by-country comparison of total Defense Investment spending and associated growth trajectories. It offers two separate data points for each country: triangles depict the absolute size of Defense Investment spending in 2005 (y-axis) and the CAGR for the 2000–2005 period (x-axis) for each respective country. The circles provide the same information for 2011 and the 2005–2011 period (unless otherwise noted). Arrows connect both data points for each country. They allow for easy reference points to determine the direction of change in Defense Investment spending in each country between both data points.

Figure 3.1. Defense Investment Spending by Country (2000–2011)

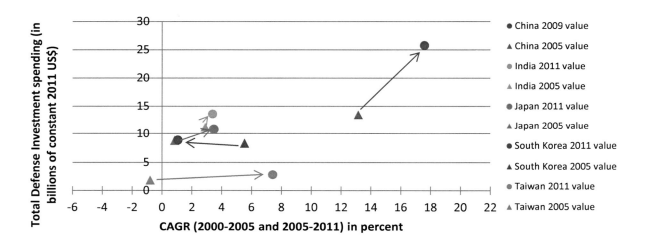

Note: For China, the second Defense Investment value is for 2009 and the second CAGR is for 2005–2009.

Sources: Chinese MoD White Papers, China's National Defense, 2002, 2004, 2006, 2008, 2010; U.S. Department of Defense 2010 Annual Report to Congress on Military and Security Developments Involving the People's Republic of China; Indian Union Budget and Economic Survey: Expenditure Budget, 2000–2013; Japanese MoD White Papers, 2005–2011; South Korean MoD White Papers, 2000, 2006, 2008, 2010; South Korean MoD; Taiwanese National Defense Report, 2009 and 2011; analysis by CSIS Defense-Industrial Initiatives Group.

---

[8] The Methodology section provides a detailed explanation for the definitions and compositions of the individual defense spending categories. It should be noted that not all countries provide sufficient details in their budget documents to allow for a breakdown into each of the categories assessed in this report. For instance, the analysis of R&D spending only covers India, Japan, and South Korea due to data limitations in the remaining two countries. In addition, for China detailed budget breakdowns are not available for the entire 2000 to 2011 time series. As a result the analysis for China can only utilize 2009 numbers, as the most recent year with a detailed budget breakdown available, when comparing it to 2011 numbers for all other countries.

In absolute terms China allocated $25.8 billion, more than any other country, to Defense Investments in 2009 (see Figure 3.1). This was commensurate with China's position as Asia's biggest overall defense spender. India was the second-largest spender on Defense Investment with around $13.6 billion in 2011, followed by Japan with almost $10.8 billion, despite the fact that Japanese defense spending in 2011 was 57.8 percent higher than the entire Indian defense budget. This can be attributed to the two countries' divergent defense priorities. India in 2011 spent 36.7 percent of its defense budget on Defense Investment—the highest relative value among the countries analyzed—while Japan allocated a group low of 18.5 percent of its defense resources to Defense Investment (see Figure 3.2). The remaining three countries—China (2009 value), South Korea, and Taiwan—all allocated in 2011 between 27.7 and 32.2 percent of their respective defense budgets to Defense Investment spending.

Figure 3.2. Defense Investment Spending as a Share of Total Defense Spending by Country (2000–2011)

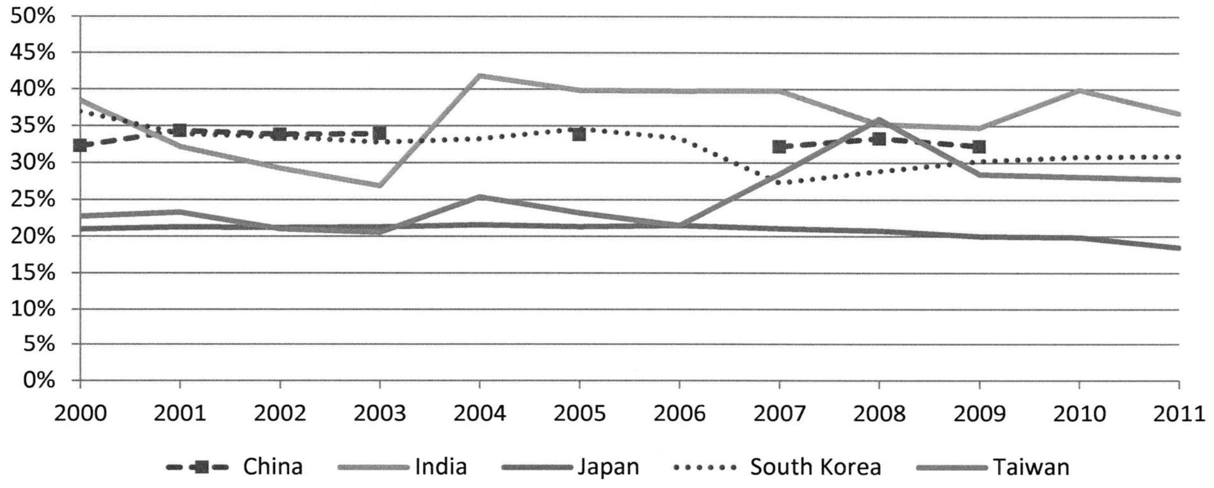

Sources: Chinese MoD White Papers, China's National Defense, 2002, 2004, 2006, 2008, 2010; U.S. Department of Defense 2010 Annual Report to Congress on Military and Security Developments Involving the People's Republic of China; Indian Union Budget and Economic Survey: Expenditure Budget, 2000–2013; Japanese MoD White Papers, 2005–2011; South Korean MoD White Papers, 2000, 2006, 2008, 2010; South Korean MoD; Taiwanese National Defense Report, 2009 and 2011; analysis by CSIS Defense-Industrial Initiatives Group.

The relative allocations of China and Japan to Defense Investment spending remained fairly constant between 2000 and 2011, though Japan's exhibited a slight downward trend starting around 2006 (see Figure 3.2). India's share of Defense Investment has been the most volatile, fluctuating between a low of 26.8 percent in 2003 and a high of 41.8 percent in 2004. From 2005 onward, India's relative allocations were more stable, ranging from 39.9 percent (2010) to 35.2 percent (2008). Taiwan increased its Defense Investment share of the defense budget from 22.7 percent in 2000 to 35.9 percent in 2008. That year, the relative size of its Defense Investment spending exceeded that of all other countries. South Korea's Defense Investment spending slowly declined in relative terms from 36.9 percent in 2000 to a low of 27.3 percent in 2007. Starting in 2008 it steadily increased to 30.9 percent in 2011.

The growth patterns of Defense Investment spending mirror developments in overall defense budgets. Defense Investment spending for all five countries increased in constant 2011 U.S. dollars during the last decade (see Table 3). With the exception of South Korea, Defense Investment accounts grew significantly faster between 2005 and 2011 than between 2000 and 2005 (see Figure 3.2). In the case of Taiwan, Defense Investment spending decreased in the first half of the decade, only to outpace that of India, South Korea, and Japan in the second half of the past decade (7.4 percent CAGR). This trend reversal was in part fueled by increases in total Taiwanese defense spending, but predominantly by a relative shift in defense budget toward the Defense Investment category.

Table 3. CAGRs for Total Defense and Defense Investment Spending in Constant 2011 U.S. Dollars by Country (2000–2011)

Countries	Defense Spending 2000–2011 CAGR	
	Total	Defense Investment
China	15.1%*	15.1%*
India	3.6%	3.2%
Japan	3.5%	2.3%
South Korea	4.8%	3.1%
Taiwan	1.8%	3.6%

* For China, CAGRs are for 2000–2009.

Sources: Chinese MoD White Papers, China's National Defense, 2002, 2004, 2006, 2008, 2010; U.S. Department of Defense 2010 Annual Report to Congress on Military and Security Developments Involving the People's Republic of China; Indian Union Budget and Economic Survey: Expenditure Budget, 2000–2013; Japanese MoD White Papers, 2005–2011; South Korean MoD White Papers, 2000, 2006, 2008, 2010; South Korean MoD; Taiwanese National Defense Report, 2009 and 2011; analysis by CSIS Defense-Industrial Initiatives Group.

Taiwan is the only case where the Defense Investment category grew at a faster pace than overall defense budgets (see Table 3). This should have enabled Taiwan to accelerate the modernization of its armed forces and defense infrastructure. It will be interesting to see whether this trend will continue in the coming years or if the relative growth of Defense Investment accounts within the defense budget has reached an upper limit due to fixed expenses on Personnel and O&M. In China, Defense Investment spending increased at the same rate as the overall defense budget. For India, Japan, and South Korea, growth of overall defense budgets outpaced gains in the Defense Investment category. This did not lead to a reduction in capital expenditures, as Defense Investment spending between 2000 and 2011 grew in all three countries. However, India, Japan, and South Korea did spend a smaller share of their growing defense budgets on Defense Investment.

Figure 3.3 provides a country-by-country comparison for the absolute size of per-soldier Defense Investment spending and associated growth trajectories. It offers two separate data points for each country. The triangles depict the absolute size of Defense Investment spending in 2005 (y-axis) and the CAGR for the 2000–2005 period (x-axis) for each respective country. The circles provide the same information for 2011 and the 2005–2011 timeframes (unless otherwise noted). Arrows connect both data points for each country. Taken together, this enables a quick determination of the direction of change for per-soldier Defense Investment spending in each country.

Figure 3.3. Per-Soldier Defense Investment Spending by Country (2005, 2011)

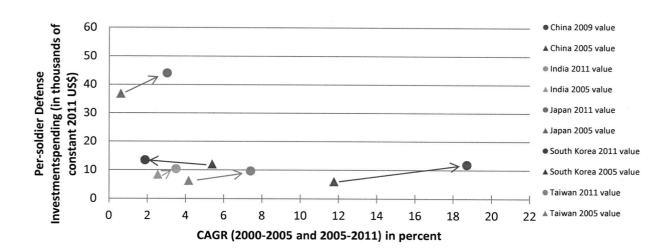

Note: For China, the second per-soldier Defense Investment value is for 2009 and the second CAGR is for 2005–2009.

Sources: Chinese MoD White Papers, China's National Defense, 2002, 2004, 2006, 2008, 2010; U.S. Department of Defense 2010 Annual Report to Congress on Military and Security Developments Involving the People's Republic of China; Indian Union Budget and Economic Survey: Expenditure Budget, 2000–2013; Japanese MoD White Papers, 2005–2011; South Korean MoD White Papers, 2000, 2006, 2008, 2010; South Korean MoD; Taiwanese National Defense Report, 2009 and 2011; IISS Military Balance; analysis by CSIS Defense-Industrial Initiatives Group.

With almost $44,100 spent per service member in 2011, Japan devoted significantly more to Defense Investment on a per-soldier basis than any of the other four Asian countries (see Figure 3.3). This is somewhat expected given the sizeable gap in overall per-soldier spending between Japan and the other countries (see chapter 1.2). However, it is noteworthy that the size of this gap was considerably smaller in the Defense Investment category. While Japan's overall per-soldier spending in 2011 was more than five times as large as the second-biggest spender in this category (South Korea), it was only three times as large as the second-biggest spender for Defense Investment spending (South Korea). This narrower gap was a direct result of the relatively smaller portion of the budget Japan allocated to Defense Investment (18.5 percent in 2011) compared to the other four countries.

Spending on Defense Investment per soldier by China, India, South Korea, and Taiwan was very similar. South Korea marked the upper bound with around $13,500 per-soldier spending for Defense Investment in 2011 and Taiwan the lower bound with approximately $9,600.

Per-soldier Defense Investment spending increased for all five countries between 2000 and 2011 (2009 in the case of China) and—with the exception of South Korea—grew at an accelerated pace between 2005 and 2011. Overall, the growth differentials between Defense Investment and per-soldier Defense Investment spending mirror the differences between total and per-soldier defense spending. For the countries that increased their force structure—China, India, and Japan—increases in per-soldier Defense Investment spending were smaller than in Defense Investment spending. Meanwhile, for South Korea and Taiwan, which decreased their troop numbers, the opposite trend occurred. For Taiwan this difference was the most noticeable: its overall Defense Investment spending contracted between 2000 and 2005 by nearly 0.8 percent CAGR, while its per-soldier Defense Investment spending exhibited a 4.2

percent CAGR, outpacing India's and Japan's growth during this timeframe. This was due to the substantial reduction in Taiwan's troop levels during 2000–2005.

3.2   Personnel

Figure 3.4 provides a country-by-country comparison for the absolute size of Personnel spending and associated growth trajectories. It offers two separate data points for each country. Triangles depict the absolute size of Personnel spending in 2005 (y-axis) and the CAGR for the 2000–2005 period (x-axis) for each respective country. Circles provide the same information for 2011 and the 2005–2011 period (unless otherwise noted). Arrows connect both data points for each country. This allows for a quick determination of the direction of change in Personnel spending by country.

Figure 3.4. Personnel Spending by Country (2005, 2011)

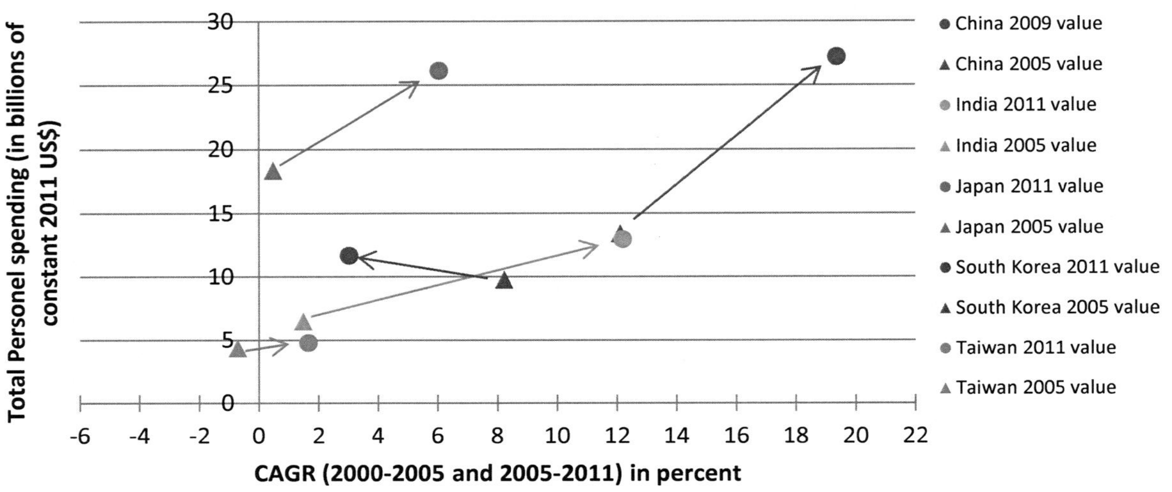

Note: For China, the second Personnel spending value is for 2009 and the second CAGR is for 2005–2009.

Sources: Chinese MoD White Papers, China's National Defense, 2002, 2004, 2006, 2008, 2010; U.S. Department of Defense 2010 Annual Report to Congress on Military and Security Developments Involving the People's Republic of China; Indian Union Budget and Economic Survey: Expenditure Budget, 2000–2013; Japanese MoD White Papers, 2005–2011; South Korean MoD White Papers, 2000, 2006, 2008, 2010; South Korean MoD; Taiwanese National Defense Report, 2009 and 2011; analysis by CSIS Defense-Industrial Initiatives Group.

In absolute terms, China and Japan spent the most on Personnel, with around $27.2 billion in 2009 and $26.1 billion in 2011, respectively (see Figure 3.4). This is noteworthy given that China's total defense spending was 64.5 percent larger than Japan's in 2009 and 54.6 percent larger in 2011. The similar amounts allocated to Personnel were due to Japan's personnel heavy budget, with 44.9 percent of the defense budget devoted to this category in 2011 compared to China's 34.0 percent in 2009 (see Figure 3.5). Among the five countries, Taiwan allocated in 2011 the highest share (47.5 percent) of its defense budget to Personnel spending, while China (2009) spent the least. In 2011, India and South Korea spent around $13.0 and $11.7 billion respectively on Personnel, representing relative budget shares of 35.0 and 40.8 percent, respectively.

Figure 3.5. Personnel Spending as a Share of Total Defense Spending by Country (2000–2011)

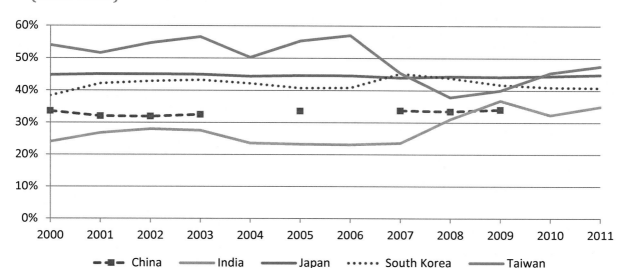

Sources: Chinese MoD White Papers, China's National Defense, 2002, 2004, 2006, 2008, 2010; U.S. Department of Defense 2010 Annual Report to Congress on Military and Security Developments Involving the People's Republic of China; Indian Union Budget and Economic Survey: Expenditure Budget, 2000–2013; Japanese MoD White Papers, 2005–2011; South Korean MoD White Papers, 2000, 2006, 2008, 2010; South Korean MoD; Taiwanese National Defense Report, 2009 and 2011; analysis by CSIS Defense-Industrial Initiatives Group.

As was the case with Defense Investment spending, China and Japan allocated relatively stable shares of their defense budget to Personnel spending between 2000 and 2011 (see Figure 3.5). Taiwan between 2000 and 2006 consistently spent more than half of its defense budget on Personnel, then reduced this category to below 50 percent before resuming a growth path to reach 47.5 percent in 2011. South Korea's allocations to Personnel spending increased moderately from 38.3 percent in 2000 to 40.8 in 2011, reaching a peak of 45.2 percent in 2007. India maintained a Personnel spending share of less than 30 percent between 2000 and 2007, which put it at the bottom of the five Asian countries for this timeframe. In 2008, its allocations to Personnel spending increased significantly to 31.1 percent and reached 35.0 percent in 2011.

Personnel spending increased for all countries between 2000 and 2011 (see Table 4). As was the case for the Defense Investment category, the second half of the decade saw more dynamic growth for all countries except South Korea. In the case of Taiwan, Personnel spending declined between 2000 and 2005 with a CAGR of negative 0.8 percent. This pattern paralleled Taiwan's overall defense spending trends.

Table 4. CAGRs for Total Defense and Personnel Spending in Constant 2011 U.S. Dollars by Country (2000–2011)

Countries	Defense Spending 2000–2011 CAGR	
	Total	**Personnel**
China	15.1%*	15.3%*
India	3.6%	7.2%
Japan	3.5%	3.5%
South Korea	4.8%	5.4%
Taiwan	1.8%	0.6%

*For China, CAGRs are for 2000–2009.

Sources: Chinese MoD White Papers, China's National Defense, 2002, 2004, 2006, 2008, 2010; U.S. Department of Defense 2010 Annual Report to Congress on Military and Security Developments Involving the People's Republic of China; Indian Union Budget and Economic Survey: Expenditure Budget, 2000–2013; Japanese MoD White Papers, 2005–2011; South Korean MoD White Papers, 2000, 2006, 2008, 2010; South Korean MoD; Taiwanese National Defense Report, 2009 and 2011; analysis by CSIS Defense-Industrial Initiatives Group.

In China, India, and South Korea, growth in Personnel spending between 2000 and 2011 outpaced growth in total defense spending (see Table 4). In Japan, increases in Personnel spending paralleled growth in total defense spending, while in Taiwan spending on Personnel grew at a slower pace than the overall defense budget.

Figure 3.6 provides a country-by-country comparison for the absolute size of per-soldier Personnel spending and associated growth trajectories. It offers two separate data points for each country. The triangles represent the absolute size of Personnel spending in 2005 (y-axis) and the CAGR for the 2000–2005 period (x-axis) for each respective country. The circles provide the same information for 2011 and the 2005–2011 period (unless otherwise noted). Arrows connect both data points for each country. This provides a snapshot of the directions of change in per-soldier Personnel spending for each country.

Figure 3.6. Per-Soldier Personnel Spending by Country (2005, 2011)

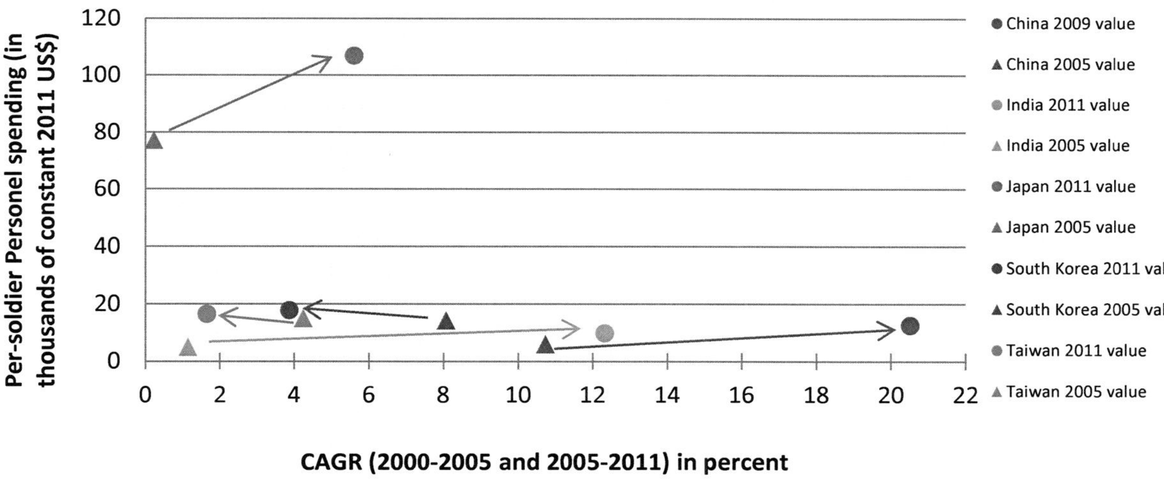

Note: For China, the second per-soldier Personnel spending value is for 2009 and the second CAGR is for 2005–2009.

Sources: Chinese MoD White Papers, China's National Defense, 2002, 2004, 2006, 2008, 2010; Department of Defense 2010 Annual Report to Congress on Military and Security Developments Involving the People's Republic of China; Indian Union Budget and Economic Survey: Expenditure Budget, 2000–2013; Japanese MoD White Papers, 2005–2011; South Korean MoD White Papers, 2000, 2006, 2008, 2010; South Korean MoD; Taiwanese National Defense Report, 2009 and 2011; IISS Military Balance; analysis by CSIS Defense-Industrial Initiatives Group.

When measuring Personnel spending on a per-soldier basis, Japan ranked the highest with $106,900 per soldier in 2011. Japan spent six times more than the second-highest spender in this category, South Korea, which spent $17,800 per soldier. India had the lowest per-soldier Personnel spending, with $9,800 in 2011 (see Figure 3.6). For per-soldier Personnel spending, the gap between Japan and the other countries was wider than for overall per-soldier spending due to Japan's personnel heavy budget.

Per-soldier Personnel spending increased for all five countries between 2000 and 2011 (2009 for China). South Korea and Taiwan increased Personnel spending at a faster rate between 2000 and 2005, with growth slowing down in the second part of the decade. For China, India, and Japan the trend was reversed, with steeper growth between 2005 and 2011. Overall, the growth differentials between Personnel and per-soldier Personnel spending resemble the differences between total and per-soldier defense spending. For the countries that increased their troop numbers—China, India, and Japan—increases in per-soldier Personnel spending were smaller than in overall Personnel spending. Meanwhile, for South Korea and Taiwan, both of which decreased their troop numbers, the opposite trend occurred. This was particularly true in Taiwan due to its substantial reduction of troop levels.

3.3   Operations and Maintenance (O&M)

Figure 3.7 provides a country-by-country comparison for the absolute size of O&M spending and associated growth trajectories. It offers two separate data points for each country. Triangles represent the absolute size of O&M spending in 2005 (y-axis) and the CAGR for the 2000–2005 period (x-axis) for each respective country. Circles provide the same information for 2011 and the years 2005–2011 (unless otherwise noted). Arrows connect the two data points for each country. This allows for an easy analysis of the direction of change for O&M spending in each country.

Figure 3.7. Operations and Maintenance Spending by Country (2005, 2011)

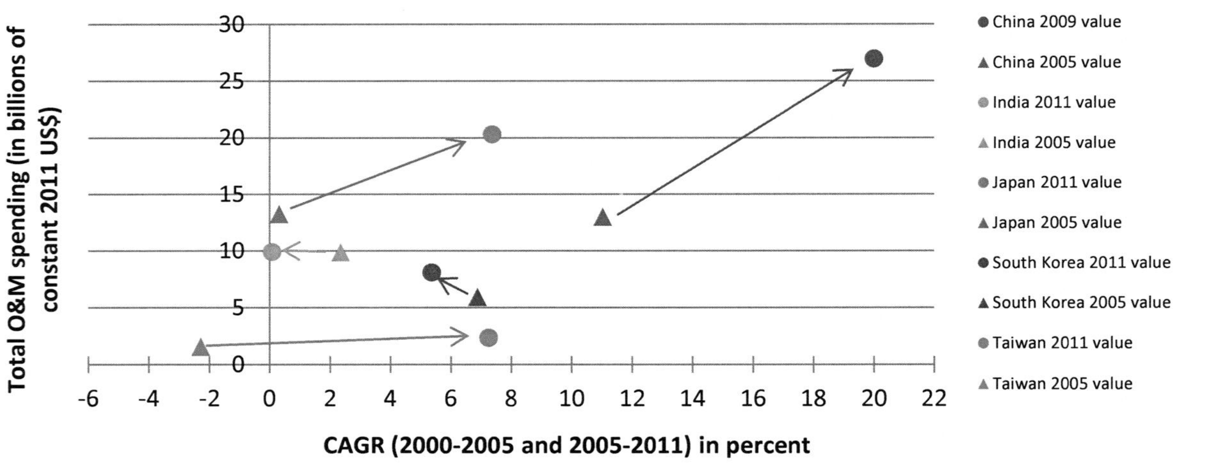

Note: For China, the second O&M value is for 2009 and the second CAGR is for 2005–2009.

Sources: Chinese MoD White Papers, China's National Defense, 2002, 2004, 2006, 2008, 2010; U.S. Department of Defense 2010 Annual Report to Congress on Military and Security Developments Involving the People's Republic of China; Indian Union Budget and Economic Survey: Expenditure Budget, 2000–2013; Japanese MoD White Papers, 2005–2011; South Korean MoD White Papers, 2000, 2006, 2008, 2010; South Korean MoD; Taiwanese National Defense Report, 2009 and 2011; analysis by CSIS Defense-Industrial Initiatives Group.

In absolute terms, China spent the most on O&M ($27.0 billion in 2009), followed by Japan ($20.3 billion in 2011) (see Figure 3.7). India and South Korea spent $9.9 and $8.1 billion, respectively, and Taiwan allocated $2.4 billion for O&M in 2011. Of all the countries analyzed, Taiwan spent the smallest share of its defense budget on O&M (23.2 percent), while Japan led the group with 34.9 percent of defense spending allocated to this category in 2011 (see Figure 3.8).

Figure 3.8. Operations and Maintenance Spending as a Share of Total Defense Spending by Country (2000–2011)

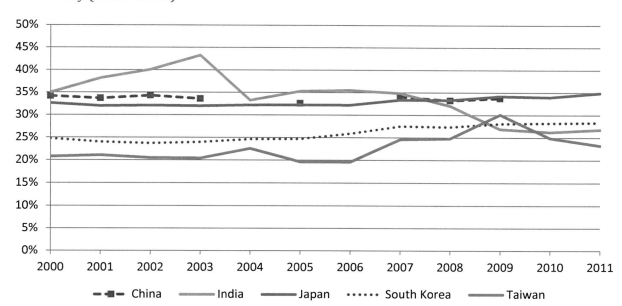

Sources: Chinese MoD White Papers, China's National Defense, 2002, 2004, 2006, 2008, 2010; U.S. Department of Defense 2010 Annual Report to Congress on Military and Security Developments Involving the People's Republic of China; Indian Union Budget and Economic Survey: Expenditure Budget, 2000–2013; Japanese MoD White Papers, 2005–2011; South Korean MoD White Papers, 2000, 2006, 2008, 2010; South Korean MoD; Taiwanese National Defense Report, 2009 and 2011; analysis by CSIS Defense-Industrial Initiatives Group.

The relative share of O&M spending in China remained stable in the years for which data are available (see Figure 3.8). The relative size of the O&M category in Japan and South Korea expanded moderately between 2000 and 2011, from 32.6 to 34.9 percent and 24.7 to 28.3 percent, respectively. In both countries, these increases were predominantly caused by growth spurts between 2006 and 2009. India had the largest O&M budget share of all five countries in 2000 with 35.0 percent, which further grew to 43.2 percent in 2003. However, it subsequently curtailed spending in this category to 26.2 percent in 2010 and 26.8 percent in 2011, making it the second-smallest O&M spender in relative terms in both years. From 2000 to 2006, Taiwan allocated between 19.6 percent (2006) and 22.4 percent (2004) of its defense budget to O&M spending. Starting in 2007, the share of O&M spending began to grow significantly, peaking at 30.1 percent in 2009, at which point it exceeded the relative size of the Indian and South Korean O&M budget. After 2009, Taiwan again reduced its relative O&M allocations, reaching 23.2 percent in 2011.

Between 2000 and 2011, O&M spending increased in all countries. For China, Japan, and Taiwan, growth was higher between 2005 and 2011 than during the previous five years. Japan experienced almost no growth in O&M spending between 2000 and 2005, and Taiwan's O&M account shrank during this timeframe. However, between 2005 and 2011 both countries exhibited robust CAGRs of 7.4 and 7.3 percent, respectively. For India and South Korea, growth in O&M spending slowed in the 2005–2011 period. India's spending on O&M was virtually flat during this timeframe (CAGR of 0.1 percent).

Table 5. CAGRs for Total Defense and Operations and Maintenance Spending in Constant 2011 U.S. Dollars by Country (2000–2011)

Countries	Defense Spending 2000–2011 CAGR	
	Total	O&M
China	15.1%*	14.9%*
India	3.6%	1.1%
Japan	3.5%	4.1%
South Korea	4.8%	6.1%
Taiwan	1.8%	2.8%

* For China, CAGRs are for 2000–2009.

Sources: Chinese MoD White Papers, China's National Defense, 2002, 2004, 2006, 2008, 2010; U.S. Department of Defense 2010 Annual Report to Congress on Military and Security Developments Involving the People's Republic of China; Indian Union Budget and Economic Survey: Expenditure Budget, 2000–2013; Japanese MoD White Papers, 2005–2011; South Korean MoD White Papers, 2000, 2006, 2008, 2010; South Korean MoD; Taiwanese National Defense Report, 2009 and 2011; analysis by CSIS Defense-Industrial Initiatives Group.

For Japan, South Korea, and Taiwan, growth in O&M spending outpaced growth in total defense budgets (see Table 5). In Taiwan, both the Defense Investment and O&M categories grew at a faster rate than total defense, likely a result of substantial reductions in Taiwan's force structure (see chapter 1.2). In India, O&M spending increased more slowly than total defense spending, while Personnel spending grew at a faster rate.

Figure 3.9 provides a country-by-country comparison for the absolute size of per-soldier O&M spending and associated growth trajectories. It offers two separate data points for each country. The triangles depict the absolute size of O&M spending in 2005 (y-axis) and the CAGR for the 2000–2005 period (x-axis) for each respective country. The circles provide the same information for 2011 and the years 2005–2011 (unless otherwise noted). Arrows connect both data points for each country, thereby providing a snapshot of change for per-soldier O&M spending in each country.

Figure 3.9. Per-Soldier Operations and Maintenance Spending by Country (2005, 2011)

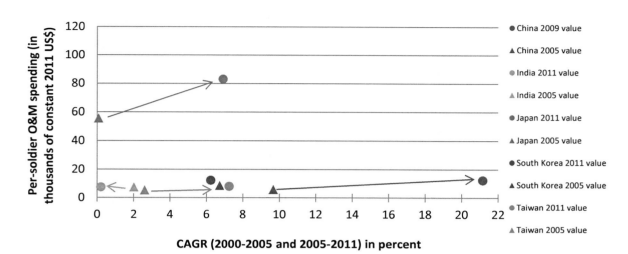

Note: For China, the second O&M per-soldier value is for 2009 and the second CAGR is for 2005–2009.

Sources: Chinese MoD White Papers, China's National Defense, 2002, 2004, 2006, 2008, 2010; U.S. Department of Defense 2010 Annual Report to Congress on Military and Security Developments Involving the People's Republic of China; Indian Union Budget and Economic Survey: Expenditure Budget, 2000–2013; Japanese MoD White Papers, 2005–2011; South Korean MoD White Papers, 2000, 2006, 2008, 2010; South Korean MoD; Taiwanese National Defense Report, 2009 and 2011; IISS Military Balance; analysis by CSIS Defense-Industrial Initiatives Group.

Japan's per-soldier spending on O&M exceeded that of the other four countries by a considerable margin. In 2011, Japan spent $83,100 per soldier on O&M compared to between $7,500 (India) and $12,400 (China, 2009 value) for other countries (see Figure 3.9). Japan thus spent almost seven times more than the second-biggest spender in this category. The per-soldier spending gap between Japan and the other countries was therefore the widest in the case of O&M, as Japan allocated a greater share of its defense budget to O&M than any other country.

Per-soldier O&M spending increased for all five countries between 2000 and 2011. With the exception of India and South Korea, it grew at an accelerated pace between 2005 and 2011. Overall, the growth differentials between total O&M and per-soldier O&M spending mirror the differences between total and per-soldier defense spending. For the countries that increased their force structure—China, India, and Japan—increases in per-soldier O&M spending were smaller than in O&M spending. Meanwhile, for South Korea and Taiwan, both of which decreased their troop numbers, the opposite trend occurred. Taiwan's total O&M spending contracted between 2000 and 2005, while its per-soldier O&M spending exhibited a 2.6 percent CAGR, outpacing India's and Japan's growth in O&M spending during this timeframe.

3.4 Defense Research and Development (R&D)

Figure 3.10 provides a country-by-country comparison for the absolute size of Defense R&D spending and associated growth trajectories for the three countries for which Defense R&D expenditure data are available. The figure presents two separate data points for each country: triangles depict the absolute size of Defense R&D spending in 2005 (y-axis) and the CAGR for the 2000–2005 period (x-axis) for each respective country; circles provide the same information for 2011 and the 2005–2011 period (unless otherwise noted). Arrows connect both data points for each country. The figure thus allows for a quick determination of the direction in which Defense R&D spending in each country has changed in the past decade.

Figure 3.10. Defense Research and Development Spending by Country (2005, 2011)

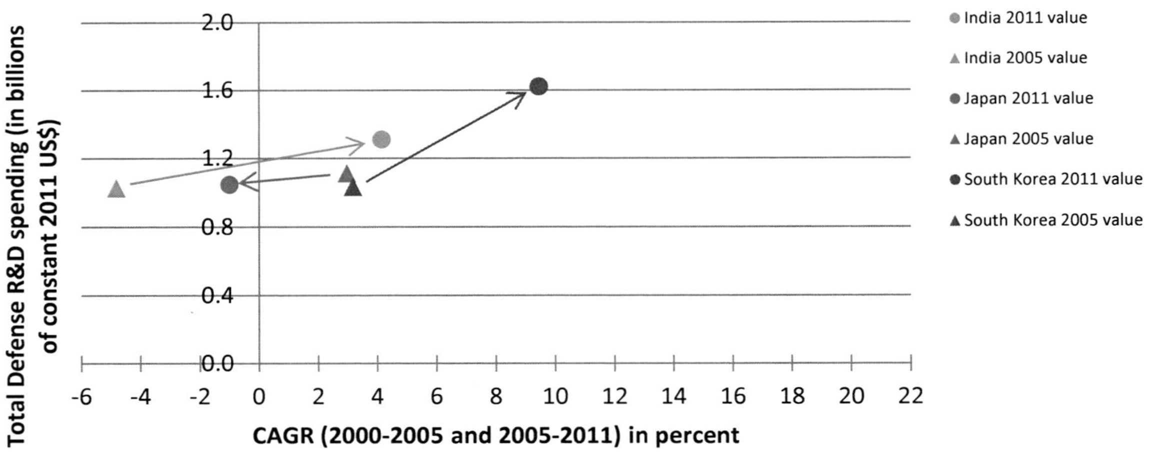

Note: For South Korea, the second R&D value is for 2010 and the second CAGR is for 2005–2010.

Sources: Indian Union Budget and Economic Survey: Expenditure Budget, 2000–2013; Japanese MoD White Papers, 2005–2011; South Korean MoD White Papers, 2000, 2006, 2008, 2010; South Korean MoD; analysis by CSIS Defense-Industrial Initiatives Group.

In this report, Defense R&D spending is a subcomponent of the Defense Investment spending category.[9] Of the three countries for which Defense R&D spending data are available, South Korea spent the most in absolute terms with $1.6 billion in 2010 followed by India and Japan with $1.3 and $1.0 billion in 2011, respectively (see Figure 3.10). South Korea's Defense R&D spending represented a 6.1 percent share of its defense budget in 2010, and India's and Japan's contributions accounted for 3.5 and 1.8 percent of their defense budgets in 2011 (see Figure 3.11).

---

[9] The Methodology appendix provides detailed definitions for the spending categories used in this report.

Figure 3.11. Defense Research and Development Spending as a Share of Total Defense Spending by Country (2000–2011)

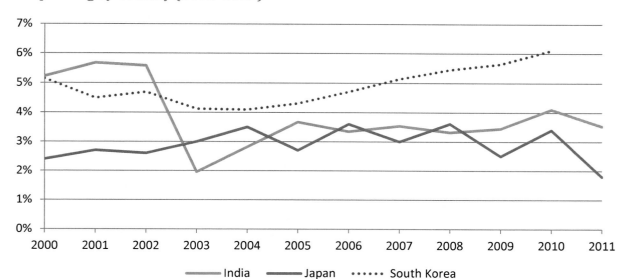

Sources: Chinese MoD White Papers, China's National Defense, 2002, 2004, 2006, 2008, 2010; U.S. Department of Defense 2010 Annual Report to Congress on Military and Security Developments Involving the People's Republic of China; Indian Union Budget and Economic Survey: Expenditure Budget, 2000–2013; Japanese MoD White Papers, 2005–2011; South Korean MoD White Papers, 2000, 2006, 2008, 2010; South Korean MoD; Taiwanese National Defense Report, 2009 and 2011; analysis by CSIS Defense-Industrial Initiatives Group.

South Korea's budget for Defense R&D declined in relative terms from 5.1 percent of the defense budget in 2000 to 4.1 percent in 2004 (see Figure 3.11). Starting in 2005, the share of Defense R&D increased steadily, peaking at 6.1 percent in 2010. The relative share of Japan's Defense R&D spending has been heavily influenced by annual fluctuations, ranging from a low of 2.4 percent in 2000 to a high of 3.6 percent in 2008, and dipping below the 2 percent threshold for the first time in 2011 (1.8 percent). Between 2000 and 2002, India maintained Defense R&D spending in excess of 5 percent of its defense budget. In 2003, the share of Defense R&D dropped sharply to 2.0 percent, but subsequently increased again between 2003 and 2005 and has since fluctuated between 3.3 percent (2008) and 4.1 percent (2010).

India's total Defense R&D spending stayed virtually flat between 2000 and 2011 (see Table 6), while Japan experienced modest growth with a 0.8 percent CAGR. South Korea exhibited the most significant increases during this period, with a CAGR of 6.3 percent, with most of the growth occurring between 2005 and 2011 (9.5 percent CAGR during this timeframe compared to a 3.2 percent CAGR during the previous five years). Japan's Defense R&D spending increased by a 3.0 percent CAGR between 2000 and 2005 and then contracted by a negative 1.0 percent CAGR in the subsequent six years. In India's case, Defense R&D spending shrunk during the first half of the decade with a negative 4.8 percent CAGR, only to grow at the rate of 4.2 percent per year between 2005 and 2011.

Table 6. CAGRs for Total Defense and Defense Research and Development Spending in Constant 2011 U.S. Dollars by Country (2000–2011)

Countries	Defense Spending 2000–2011 CAGR	
	Total	Defense R&D
India	3.6%	0.0%
Japan	3.5%	0.8%
South Korea	4.5%*	6.3%*

* For South Korea, the R&D spending CAGR is for 2000–2010.

Sources: Indian Union Budget and Economic Survey: Expenditure Budget, 2000–2013; Japanese MoD White Papers, 2005–2011; South Korean MoD White Papers, 2000, 2006, 2008, 2010; South Korean MoD; analysis by CSIS Defense-Industrial Initiatives Group.

Of the countries analyzed in this report, only in South Korea did Defense R&D spending grow at a faster rate than total defense spending. While Defense R&D spending is an input rather than an output metric, South Korea's spending may be indicative of more home-grown capabilities in the future. In Japan, Defense R&D allocations grew at a slower rate compared to total defense spending, and in India, they did not grow at all.

Figure 3.12 provides a country-by-country comparison for absolute size of per-soldier Defense R&D spending and growth trajectories for countries for which Defense R&D expenditure data are available. The y-axis provides spending in billions for years 2005 and 2011, while the x-axis shows the CAGRs of this defense spending category. The figure offers two separate data points for each country: triangles depict the absolute size of Defense R&D spending in 2005 (y-axis) and the CAGR for the 2000–2005 period (x-axis) for each respective country, and circles provide the same information for 2011 and the 2005–2011 period (unless otherwise noted). Arrows connect both data points for each country and represent the direction of change in per-soldier Defense R&D spending in each country.

Figure 3.12. Per-Soldier Defense Research and Development Spending by Country (2005, 2011)

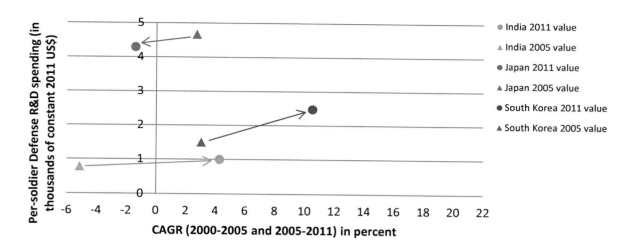

Note: For South Korea, the second R&D per-soldier value is for 2010 and the second CAGR is for 2005–2010.

Sources: Indian Union Budget and Economic Survey: Expenditure Budget, 2000–2013; Japanese MoD White Papers, 2005–2011; South Korean MoD White Papers, 2000, 2006, 2008, 2010; South Korean MoD; IISS Military Balance; analysis by CSIS Defense-Industrial Initiatives Group.

With around $4,300 per service member, Japan spent more on Defense R&D on a per-soldier basis than South Korea and India with some $2,500 and $1,000, respectively (see Figure 3.12). Defense R&D therefore constituted the spending category with the smallest per-soldier spending gap between Japan and the other countries. The generally higher level of per-soldier spending in Japan was therefore diminished for Defense R&D due to Japan's comparatively low level of spending in this category.

Between 2000 and 2011 (2010 in the case of South Korea), per-soldier Defense R&D spending increased in South Korea and Japan but slightly decreased in India. In South Korea, per-soldier Defense R&D spending grew at a faster rate between 2005 and 2011. Mirroring developments in overall Defense R&D spending, Indian per-soldier Defense R&D spending contracted between 2000 and 2005 but grew between 2005 and 2011. For Japan, the opposite holds true.

Growth trends in Defense R&D spending and per-soldier Defense R&D spending resemble those in total and per-soldier defense spending. For the countries that increased their troop levels—India and Japan—increases in per-soldier Defense R&D spending were smaller than in Defense R&D spending. This explains why India, which experienced flat growth in Defense R&D spending, saw negative growth in per-soldier Defense R&D spending. Meanwhile South Korea, which decreased its troop numbers, experienced faster growth in per-soldier Defense R&D spending than in total Defense R&D spending.

4. Key Findings and Areas for Further Research

This section combines the analysis from the preceding sections and presents two key findings that arise. In addition, this section provides key indicators for future developments, which will determine whether the Asian defense market will continue on its current trajectory. It closes with suggestions for future research.

4.1   Accelerated Defense Spending Growth in 2005–2011

Analyzing defense spending in China, Japan, India, South Korea, and Taiwan for the years 2000 to 2011 reveals a fairly homogenous growth trend at both the aggregate and country-by-country level. Notably, defense spending during the first half of the decade (2000–2005) increased at a slower rate—even contracted in the case of Taiwan—than in the second half (2005–2011) for all countries except South Korea. Combined totals for defense spending are particularly illustrative of this trend as spending grew at nearly half the rate between 2000 and 2005 (4.5 percent CAGR) than it did in the second half of the time period (8.0 percent CAGR). Deviating from this trend of accelerated spending, South Korea's defense budget increased at a CAGR of 3.0 percent during 2005 to 2011, which was less than half its CAGR in the first half of the time period (6.9 percent). This was primarily caused by a steep growth spurt around the midpoint of the decade followed by years of slower growth. Exchange rate fluctuations further amplified this pattern.

In comparison, aggregate spending in the United States and Europe reflected a different trend. Specifically, total defense spending in the United States grew by twice as much during 2000 to 2005 (7.2 percent CAGR) as it did between 2005 and 2011 (3.6 percent CAGR). In Europe, total defense spending declined from 2001 to 2005 at a CAGR of -1.4 percent, and declined at an even faster rate (-2.5 percent CAGR) between 2006 and 2011.

This trend of accelerated defense spending beginning in 2005 begs the question: will this development continue, and if so, for how long? The answer to these questions hinges primarily upon political and economic developments. Notable political factors could include China's continued defense build-up and its posture toward the United States and Taiwan, as well as its mounting tension with Japan in the South and East China Seas. The defense outlook for South Korea and India will also continue to be largely shaped by their strained relations with North Korea and Pakistan, respectively. Notable economic factors include the availability of financial resources and the overall economic climate. The impact of the 2008 financial crisis, which continued through 2012, illustrates this fact. Although Asia was less affected by the recession compared to the United States and Europe, countries such as India, South Korea, and Taiwan all experienced some decreases in GDP growth. A worsening global economic climate, particularly in Europe, may further affect Asian economic growth and reduce the ability of governments to maintain current trends in defense spending.

Exchange rate fluctuations can also influence defense trends in Asia. Countries might capitalize on the further devaluation of the U.S. dollar against local currencies, and the resulting growth in buying power might entice these countries to increase imports of U.S. made defense capabilities. Note that this will not apply to China, which cannot procure U.S. defense goods and services, and might be diluted in countries that prioritize the development of an indigenous industrial base supporting defense, such as India.

4.2 Prioritizing Quantity over Quality

Three of the five countries assessed in this report—China, India, and Japan—ranked in the global top ten defense spenders in 2011.[10] In addition, defense spending has been on a growth trajectory in all five countries over the last decade. Between 2000 and 2011, the aggregated defense budgets of China, India, Japan, South Korea, and Taiwan have almost doubled, with much of the growth occurring in the second half of the last decade.

In parallel, three of the five countries analyzed in this report—China, India and South Korea—ranked in the global top ten in number of active troops. As a result, defense spending per soldier in these countries has consistently been relatively low. China, India, South Korea, and Taiwan spent between $28,200 and $43,600 per service member in 2011. [Japan is the exception with $238,100 spent per soldier in 2011.] By comparison, European states spent on aggregate $140,400 per service member in 2010 and the United States $504,800 per soldier in 2011. On a per-soldier basis, China, India, South Korea, and Taiwan spent as much as countries like Romania ($29,100 in 2011) or Cyprus ($44,600 in 2011). However, China alone fielded in 2011 almost as many troops as all of Europe combined yet spent only 26.6 percent of what European states spend collectively on defense that year.

While still relatively low in 2011, per soldier spending in Asia has been on the rise for the last decade as a result of higher defense budgets combined with little change in the force size of four of the five countries analyzed here. [Taiwan is the exception in this regard, having implemented a series of force reform programs that resulted in a 21.6 percent reduction in troop numbers between 2000 and 2011.[11]] As a result, growth rates in per-soldier spending resemble those in total defense spending, when measured in constant 2011 U.S. dollars (see Table 2).

Per-soldier defense spending constitutes a proxy variable for force quality as it measures the resources available for an individual soldier to be recruited, trained, compensated, equipped, and sustained. It does not, however, capture other relevant qualitative factors such as doctrine, leadership, operational experience, or how efficiently and effectively available resources are utilized. However, the comparatively low-levels of per-soldier spending in four of the five Asian countries analyzed here implies that these countries prioritize force size over force quality.

Certain conjunctures might suggest a different perspective to this assertion. Comparing per-soldier spending levels across the five Asian countries and with United States and Europe might create a distorted picture. For instance, the conscription forces of South Korea and Taiwan probably accrue a fraction of the per-soldier Personnel costs than their all-volunteer counterparts in the United States, most of Europe, or Japan. In this regard, it will be interesting to see how Taiwan will manage the transition away from conscription. Lower wage levels in China and India might narrow the buying power gaps in per-soldier Personnel spending for these two countries. Furthermore, acquiring and maintaining equipment that has been either sourced domestically or from non-Western sources might be more affordable than Western options. This is especially relevant for China and India with their strong reliance on Russian imports and growing emphasis on domestically manufactured equipment.

Nevertheless, the significant gap in per soldier defense spending between China, India, South Korea, and Taiwan and the major European militaries and the United States suggests, at least to some extent, differences in the quality of military forces. It remains to be seen if this issue will be addressed given the increase in Asian defense budgets. One potential response could be to modernize different elements of the armed forces at significantly varying speeds, effectively leading to a "high-low" force quality mix. In

---

[10] Stockholm International Peace Research Institute (2011), *SIPRI Yearbook 2011*.
[11] For information on the "Jing-shi Program," the "Jing-jin Program," and the "Jing-Tsui Program," see Section 2.5.

this model, a larger share of resources is devoted to certain high-value units providing them with, among other things, better and more frequent training and more modern equipment. Concurrently, other units receive fewer resources and are equipped with older or even outdated and obsolete equipment.

While this practice of discriminating between individual units is prevalent in any military to a certain degree, the internal gap might be more pronounced in countries such as China, India, South Korea, and Taiwan given their comparatively low per-soldier spending in conjunction with the ambition to field high-end capabilities. For instance, by Western standards China still has large numbers of obsolete aircraft in its inventory while at the same time operating state-of-the-art fighter aircrafts (in much smaller numbers) and developing an indigenous 5th generation fighter. Similarly, South Korea continues to field main battle tanks designed in the 1950s alongside new models that entered service as recently as 2010.

It remains to be seen whether Asian states will continue to field large militaries or if they will eventually follow trends in Europe and the United States, where force structure is reduced in favor of higher quality forces. Ample trade space is certainly available in China, India, and South Korea. Yet security and other political considerations might make this course of action unviable for the foreseeable future.

4.3   Key Indicators for Future Developments

The data and findings presented in this report are based on trends observed in the past decade, and given little change to the data, the findings will continue to be relevant. However, it is worth highlighting some indicators that bear watching in the near term.

Overall, continued or increasing tensions in the Asia-Pacific region could drive further increases in defense spending by Asian countries. Should the economic climate of the Asia-Pacific region concurrently show positive growth, many countries will also have increased means to respond to security concerns. On the other hand, if the financial situation in the coming years proves to be more austere, pressure on defense spending may also mount.

A continued rise in total defense spending without further increases in troop levels would raise per-soldier defense spending levels and therefore also the potential quality of national militaries. Yet such an increase would occur at a gradual pace. Elevating per-soldier spending more significantly would require cuts in force structure. Hence, announcements of major force reduction programs, such as those undertaken by Taiwan in the 1990s and 2000s, would constitute a critical precursor for a potential shift of focus toward smaller, more capable armed forces.

On the other hand, maintaining the current approach of fielding forces with a relative wide range of quality and readiness levels would manifest itself in fairly stable force structures, investments in a small number of cutting-edge systems, and the maintaining of older equipment in substantial numbers. An indicator of this would be announcements of small buys or production runs of high-end capabilities and investments in maintaining large fleets of legacy platforms.

4.4   Areas for Further Research

This report focuses on overall and functional defense spending trends for the five biggest Asian defense spenders: China, India, Japan, Taiwan, and South Korea. The research team acknowledges that focusing on five key actors does not allow for a holistic assessment of defense trends for the entire Asian region. Subsequent efforts could widen the scope and cover ASEAN member states and/or include peripheral actors like Russia, Australia, and New Zealand. Such an expansion would facilitate a more comprehensive and integrated analysis of defense trends in Asia. However, one key requirement for any follow-on research is the availability of reliable data, which may not exist for all countries.

Additional assessments of defense import and export patterns of Asian countries could enhance the understanding of sourcing streams utilized for satisfying regional force modernization requirements. An analysis on what portions of acquisition activities are indigenous or foreign sourced and identifying key importers and exporters would provide valuable insights on the Asian defense market and business opportunities in it.

Similarly, research on the regulatory frameworks governing defense acquisition and the supporting defense industrial bases in individual countries would provide a better understanding of the legal framework in which market participants operate. This would allow for more complete defense market profiles of individual countries.

A thorough understanding of defense markets should include an analysis of the industrial bases supporting defense. Such an analysis would highlight the overall structure of the defense industry, its financial health and competitiveness, its core areas of expertise, and the policy framework within which it operates.

The Defense-Industrial Initiatives Group at CSIS will continue to monitor and analyze Asian defense trends and potentially expand the scope of its effort along the lines outlined above.

Appendix A: Methodology

Scope of the Study

The countries analyzed in this study were chosen based on the size of their defense expenditures. China, India, Japan, South Korea, and Taiwan constitute the five largest spenders on defense in the Asian region, not including Russia and Australia. These five countries accounted for approximately 87 percent of total defense spending in Asia in 2011.[12] Analyzing and comparing these five countries therefore captures the key actors and trends for the Asian defense environment.

Data Sources

The data presented in this report are collected from national government documents, primarily defense budgets and white papers. These data are supplemented by data from independent sources such as Bloomberg, the International Institute for Strategic Studies (IISS), the International Monetary Fund (IMF), the Stockholm International Peace Research Institute (SIPRI), and the United Nations (UN). Integrating sources from different countries with varying accounting standards into a consistent analytical framework posed many challenges. To the extent possible, CSIS tried to apply uniform accounting and analysis standards to ensure the validity of any cross-country comparisons and associated trends identified. The Data Analysis and Defense Spending Categories sections below describe these standards and any deviations from them.

Data Analysis

The lack of a centralized data source for all Asian defense spending creates several analytical challenges. In order to conduct a comparative study and to capture only real-term effects, all data collected were converted into constant 2011 U.S. dollars. Therefore, most of the numbers presented in the respective charts and tables will not correspond to the raw data in the original sources. The CSIS Defense-Industrial Initiatives Group used Bloomberg for exchange rate conversions and the *World Economic Outlook* report of the IMF for inflation adjustments. It should be noted that utilizing constant 2011 U.S. dollars as the uniform metric for measuring defense spending in these countries alters some of the observed trends due to variations in the exchange rates between local currencies and the U.S. dollar. The authors have highlighted these currency-infused differences in the report where appropriate and in some cases also presented data in local currencies.

In addition, the data for China, India, and South Korea presented unique challenges, as outlined below.

China:

Topline figures are available for all years from the official Chinese defense white papers released every alternate year starting in 2002. However, breakdowns into functional categories are only available for the year prior to the release of the white paper. Thus, there are no official data for category breakdowns in 2004, 2006, 2010, or 2011. In addition, there are no data in the white paper for 2008 category breakdowns; for this report, these are drawn from China's submission of their military expenditure to the United Nations in 2009. In addition, many analysts posit that Chinese official sources do not capture Chinese defense spending in its entirety. To reflect this sentiment, CSIS also included estimates by SIPRI

---

[12] Stockholm International Peace Research Institute (2011), *SIPRI Yearbook 2011*.This does not include the Middle East, Oceania, and Russia.

on China's defense spending section. The U.S. Department of Defense also publishes estimates for Chinese military spending; however, a complete time series of these estimates is unavailable.

India:

The official Indian defense budget consists of the following six subcomponents: army, navy, air force, defense capital outlays, defense ordnance factories, and research and development. The analysis in this report deviated from this categorization and excluded expenditure on ordnance factories, as well as any line items in the five remaining budget documents that relate to ordnance factories. These items were excluded because they do not align with any of the categories listed in the report and are not included in any of the other country budgets. Any line items classified as revenue receipts were also excluded from the assessment. In addition, CSIS used revised estimates rather than actual expenditure for time series consistency, since actual expenditure numbers are only provided starting in 2009.

South Korea:

South Korea posed a unique challenge with regard to categorization and labeling of available data. In its government's white papers, specific line items in the defense budgets are classified into different defense spending categories in different years. Due to a lack of explanation for this reclassification, inferences were made as to which items are included in which categories.

Presumably, a reclassification of Defense Capacity Improvement (DCI) costs was carried out in conjunction with the creation of the Defense Acquisition Program Agency (DAPA) in 2006. It is inferred that after 2006 more stringent rules governed what could be classified under the DCI budget costs category. This is corroborated by the severe drop in the DCI budget between 2006 and 2007.

Spending on food and clothing varied significantly each year. In the interest of ensuring consistency of analysis, this study reclassified food and clothing to ensure they remain in the same categories for the longest continuous time period possible. This reclassification was done when food and clothing expenses were provided as a specific line item, allowing for it to be transferred to another budget category for certain years. As a result, food and clothing expenses are subsumed under O&M spending for the 2000 to 2006 period. Starting in 2007 they are included in Personnel spending.

Defense Spending Categories

The functional spending categories used in this report (Defense Investment, O&M, Personnel, Defense R&D, Defense Procurement, and "Other") mirror those used in the U.S. defense budget. These categories constitute the basic analytical framework for assessing the defense spending trends of the five Asian countries evaluated in this report. Table 7 below delineates what is included in each CSIS category, based on the U.S. budget, as well as the analytical frameworks used in previous CSIS reports.

All categories are mutually exclusive with the exception of Defense R&D and Defense Procurement, which combined constitute Defense Investment. Defense R&D is included as a separate category in the functional budget analysis in Section 3 as it indicates the degree to which a country invests in future domestic defense capabilities. However, separate data on Defense R&D expenditure are only available for India, Japan, and South Korea, with South Korea's expenditure available only through 2010. Data for China and Taiwan did not allow for a further breakdown of Defense Investment spending into Defense Procurement and Defense R&D accounts. Thus, the functional analysis of Defense R&D data in this report is limited to India, Japan, and South Korea. The section on Defense Investment for these countries includes their Defense R&D expenditure to allow consistent comparisons with China and Taiwan.

Table 7. CSIS Defense Spending Categories

CSIS Category	Breakdown
Defense Investment	Procurement and R&D
O&M	O&M and Military Construction
Personnel	Personnel, also including basic provisions such as food and clothing
Defense R&D	R&D
Defense Procurement	Procurement
Other	Placeholder

Sources: U.S. Department of Defense, Office of the Under Secretary of Defense (Comptroller); analysis by CSIS Defense-Industrial Initiatives Group.

Despite the best efforts of the research team to align the accounting practices of the individual countries with the above mentioned accounting framework, several deviations remain since the defense budget data do not offer sufficient detail to enable the redistribution of specific line items to match the standardized framework. Table 8 summarizes these deviations. The "not applicable" (N/A) designation means that no deviations from the CSIS defense spending categories were encountered.

Table 8. Defense Spending Categories Deviations

	Defense Investment	O&M	Personnel	Defense R&D	Other
China	Includes maintenance, transportation and storage of weaponry and equipment	Does not include maintenance, transportation and storage of weaponry and equipment	N/A	No separate breakdown available	N/A
India	N/A				
Japan	Includes material purchases	Does not include material purchases	N/A	N/A	N/A
South Korea	N/A				
Taiwan	N/A	N/A	N/A	No separate breakdown available	N/A

Sources: Chinese MoD White Papers, China's National Defense, 2002, 2004, 2006, 2008, 2010; Japanese MoD White Papers, 2005–2011; analysis by CSIS Defense-Industrial Initiatives Group.

About the Authors

David J. Berteau is senior vice president and director of the CSIS International Security Program, covering defense management, programs, contracting, and acquisition. His group also assesses national security economics and industry. Mr. Berteau is also an adjunct professor at Georgetown University, a director of the Procurement Round Table, and a fellow of the National Academy of Public Administration and the Robert S. Strauss Center at the University of Texas. Prior to joining CSIS, he was director of national defense and homeland security for Clark & Weinstock, director of Syracuse University's National Security Studies Program, and a senior vice president at Science Applications International Corporation (SAIC). He served in the U.S. Defense Department under four defense secretaries, including four years as principal deputy assistant secretary of defense for production and logistics. Mr. Berteau graduated with a B.A. from Tulane University in 1971 and received his master's degree in 1981 from the LBJ School of Public Affairs at the University of Texas.

Guy Ben-Ari is a deputy director and senior fellow with the Defense-Industrial Initiatives Group at CSIS, where he studies the links among innovation, industry, military capabilities and defense policy. Prior to joining CSIS, he was a research associate at George Washington University's Center for International Science and Technology Policy, where he worked on national research and development policies and network-centric capabilities. From 2000 to 2002, he managed collaborative research and development programs for Gilat Satellite Networks Ltd., an Israeli high-technology company in the field of satellite communications, and from 1995 to 2000, he was a technology analyst for the Israeli government. He has also consulted for the European Commission and the World Bank on innovation policy and project evaluation. Mr. Ben-Ari holds an M.A. in international science and technology policy from the George Washington University and a B.A. in political science from Tel Aviv University

Priscilla Hermann is a research assistant with the Defense-Industrial Initiatives Group (DIIG) at CSIS. She has contributed to various DIIG projects and coauthored a report commissioned by the European Union on the regulatory environments for homeland security in the United States and the European Union. Before joining CSIS, she was an intern for the Global Initiatives and Outreach Program at Student World Assembly, a New York–based nongovernmental organization committed to promoting democracy, human rights, and student activism worldwide. Ms. Hermann holds a B.A. with a double major in international affairs (concentrating in international economics and Europe/Eurasia) and in French language and literature from the George Washington University. She also obtained an international diploma from the Institut d'Etudes Politiques de Paris (Sciences Po), speaks fluent French, and spent two years living and studying in France.

Joachim Hofbauer is a fellow with the Defense-Industrial Initiatives Group at the Center for Strategic and International Studies (CSIS). He specializes in U.S. and European defense acquisition and industrial base issues and their impact on the transatlantic defense market. Before joining CSIS, Mr. Hofbauer worked as a defense analyst in Germany and the United Kingdom. His analysis has been published in several U.S. and German defense publications. Mr. Hofbauer holds a B.A. in European studies from the University of Passau and an M.A. with honors in security studies, with a concentration in defense analysis, from Georgetown University

Sneha Raghavan is a research assistant with the Defense-Industrial Initiatives Group. Previously, she served as a senior research assistant with AidData, a development finance database at the College of William and Mary. She holds a B.A. from the College of William and Mary with honors in international relations, where she completed a study on the effects of U.S. foreign aid on nuclear proliferation outcomes of recipient countries.